Understanding

the

Time Zones

of God

Understanding
the
Time Zones
of God

John Tetsola

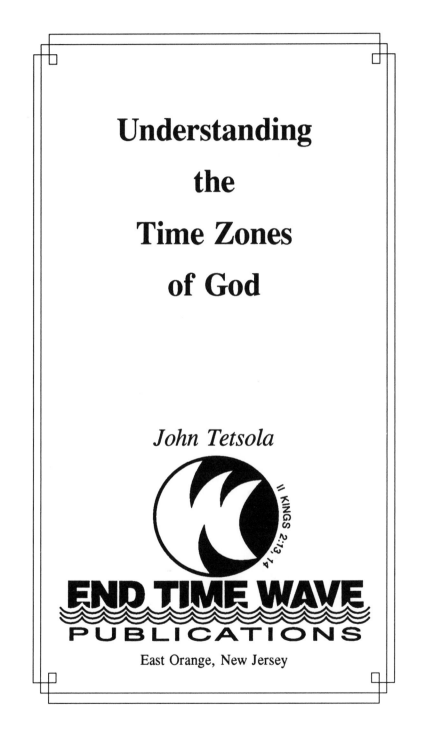

END TIME WAVE
PUBLICATIONS

East Orange, New Jersey

Understanding the Time Zones of God

ISBN 0-9634306-1-0

Designer: Izzy Sanabria
Typesetter: Nilsa Baskerville
Proofreader: Joseph G. Simon

Dedication

This book is dedicated to Apostle (Dr.) Ernest Leonard, founder, president and overseer of Victory Church Provision of Promise Ministries — for his teachings, his prophetic confrontation, his patience, his love and his understanding towards my wife (Vickie) and I while under his ministry, and for allowing us to serve as ministers under his great apostolic and prophetic mantle.

Thank you, Apostle Ernest Leonard.

Contents

Introduction

There is coming upon the Church, in this hour, a fresh new move of God. This movement will rid the Church of its grave clothes, its wilderness garments and the things that have been hindering individuals of the Body of Christ from blossoming into that man or woman of God that can be used with authority and dominion and be able to fulfill His work. This will come into existence by understanding the "Time Zones" of God.

God, in order to execute His plan, is raising up many "Unknowns" in this hour to declare the "known." In doing this, God, through His Spirit, is calling men and women to take a vow. What vow? The vow of the Nazarite — the vow of consecration, the vow of separation and the vow of holiness.

I believe that as this vow is being taken, God is causing the "hair" of the Church to grow again. I see, in the spirit, Christians all over the world, like Samson (Judges 16:21-22), crying out in this hour, "Oh God, anoint me one more time." Hallelujah! The Body of Christ has been mocked too long. The news media has disgraced the Church. But I prophesy today, as you read this book, that the "hair" of the Church is growing again. When God finishes with this prophetic Church and its leaders, we will not look the same. We might have our eyes plucked out; we may not have the fanciful clothes; we may be bloodied and limping from the warfare, but the glory is coming back home again and the Church's "hair" is growing afresh. You might be "bald," but that is alright, your spiritual hair will still grow again. And when all is said and done, the world will see the Church on the "honor roll of faith" again. Hallelujah!

For the Church to come to this point, we must stop swimming in the river where there is no power. The Church has been swimming too long in the Abana and Pharpar Rivers (II Kings 5:1-12), instead of the Jordan River. Abana means "human sufficiency," and Pharpar means "man-made help." The glory and power had been lost because the Body of Christ were dipping and dabbing in the rivers of "human sufficiency" and "human might." Jordan means "death." This is the river God wants the Church to swim in during this "Time Zone" — the river where our flesh and its works are put to death, and the spirit of man is allowed to reign supreme. When Naaman made a quality decision to dip seven times into the Jordan River, the result was a foregone conclusion. He was changed. He was new. His leprosy was healed. That is what the Spirit of God will do in this hour. He will heal men and women from their spiritual leprosy if they will dip into the Jordan River. This is what God is calling for in this "Time Zone": changed men and women, through their swimming in the Jordan River. Are you one of them? Then, join the train.

John Tetsola

Chapter I

Times and Seasons

And the wise heart will know the proper time and procedure.

Ecclesiastes 8:5b (NIV)

The Church is living in a day where many people do not know what God is doing or saying, because there is a failure in understanding the times and seasons of God. If we plan on moving with God and want to continue to work out our salvation in God's timing, then we will have to know and understand the periods of time that God has ordained for us to walk in. Now you might say, "I am comfortable in my walk;" "why do I have to know about the times and seasons of God?" or even, "things have gone well thus far, and I do not even know what times or seasons are." Well, let me say that our very lives depend upon our understanding the times and seasons of God.

And when He approached, He saw the city and wept over it,

saying, "If you had known in this day, even you, the things which make for peace! But now they have been hidden from your eyes.

For the days shall come upon you when your enemies will throw up a bank before you, and surround you, and hem you in on every side,

and will level you to the ground and your children within you, and they will not leave in you one stone upon another, because you did not recognize the time of your visitation."

Luke 19:41-44 (NASB)

1

When Jesus saw the city (Jerusalem), He wept over it. Why? Because they failed to understand the times. Let it never be said that God had not ordained that He would visit every one of us with a fresh anointing and a fresh revelation. That anointing is the presence of Jesus, and that revelation is of Jesus Himself. Israel had longed to be saved and delivered, and they were looking for a Savior. In their understanding of the timing of God, a Savior was supposed to come onto the scene and deliver them from the Roman government which was persecuting them. This Savior was supposed to come back and take over the world, in order to set up an everlasting kingdom where they would join in that reign forever. Galatians, chapter four, says, "But when the fullness of the time came, God sent forth his son ..." Now, why, if it says, "the fullness of the time," did these Jews not recognize the time of their visitation? No understanding of the time led them to any revelation as to what to do when the time came. They were supposed to receive Him but, instead, they rejected Him.

The words "times" and "seasons" are used interchangeably throughout the Bible, but they do have some distinction. Times signify duration, while seasons signify characteristics of that duration of time. A season is a time at which certain preordained events take place or necessary accomplishments need to take place, and is a regularly fixed period of time, while time involves length or measurement of moments. They both signify appointed, fixed and set times or periods. There is another word that can be interjected here, and that is "hour." It is a fixed time, or a time determined upon or demanded. Like Ecclesiastes confirms, God uses this language to speak to us about appointed and ordained times, seasons, hours and even days to accomplish His purposes on the earth.

And God said, Let there be lights in the firmament of the heaven to divide the day from the night; and let them be for signs, and for seasons, and for days, and years:

And let them be for lights in the firmament of the heaven to give light upon the earth: and it was so.

Genesis 1:14-15

God created time and seasons, and created the purposes for them. God purposed that time would show His people signs, seasons, days and years. If we do not understand time and seasons, we will not be able to understand the signs that God, Himself, is showing and putting forth concerning His movement. The Church will not be able to understand when God is moving. God is expecting His people to find out where He is going and to flow with Him. Then we can be able to understand the "timing" of God.

Now when Jesus came into the district of Caesarea Philippi, He *began* **asking His disciples, saying, "Who do people say that the Son of Man is?"**

And they said, "Some *say* **John the Baptist; and others, Elijah; but still others, Jeremiah, or one of the prophets."**

He said to them, "But who do you say that I am?"

And Simon Peter answered and said, "Thou art the Christ, the Son of the living God."

And Jesus answered and said to him, "Blessed are you, Simon Barjona, because flesh and blood did not reveal *this* **to you, but My Father who is in heaven."**

"And I also say to you that you are Peter, and upon this rock I will build My Church; and the gates of Hades shall not overpower it."

"I will give you the keys of the kingdom of heaven; and whatever you shall bind on earth shall be bound in heaven, and whatever you shall loose on earth shall be loosed in heaven."

From that time Jesus Christ began to show His disciples that He must go to Jerusalem, and suffer many things from the elders and chief priests and scribes, and be killed, and be raised upon the third day.

And Peter took Him aside and began to rebuke Him, saying, "God forbid *it*, Lord! This shall never happen to You."

But He turned and said to Peter, "Get behind Me, Satan! You are a stumbling block to Me; for you are not setting your mind on God's interest, but man's."

Matthew 16:13-19,21-23 (NASB)

Peter was one who misunderstood the "hour." Matthew tells us, here, that Peter had just received the revelation that Jesus was the Christ. It was revealed to him straight from the Father, and it was confirmed by Jesus that, based upon this revelation, the gates of hell would not prevail against the Church, but would be built upon it. The keys of the kingdom were given based upon this revelation. Then, right after that, Jesus began to reveal to his disciples about His suffering and death. In other words, Jesus was telling them about the "hour." The hour of what? The hour of redemption. It is written that Peter took Jesus to the side and began to rebuke Him, saying, "be it far from thee: this shall not be unto thee." Many things occur when we misunderstand the "hour." In our ignorance, there will always be a rebuke, a murmur, an opinion that is not in line with God. Without knowing it, we begin to speak against the ways of God, the house of God, or the man or the woman of God.

The pharisegic spirit gets on us and we spiritually start saying that, "Jesus casts out devils by Beelzebub," not knowing that it is actually by the finger of God that they flee. We start living as in Isaiah, chapter five, where it says "woe unto those that call evil good, and good evil; who substitute darkness for light and light for darkness; who substitute bitter for sweet and sweet for bitter." And this is where Peter was. We can learn something from the response that Jesus gave Peter. It says, "Get thee

4

behind Me, Satan: thou art an offense unto me: for thou savourest not the things that be of God, but those that be of men." An ignorance of an hour in your life will cause a divine purpose to be delayed or even aborted. Anytime we allow satan to cause our minds to dwell in this earthly realm, we can become a stumbling block to the divine purposes of God. The ramifications of this message are great, and that is why we need to understand it.

And he [satan] will speak out against the Most High and wear down the saints of the Highest One, and he will intend to make alterations in times and in law; and they will be given into his hand for a time, times and half a time.

Daniel 7:25 (NASB)

If the devil could get us to go swimming in the winter or skiing in the summer, then we have been taken captive by his devices. This lines up with the prophetic word of Jeremiah that says, "If you break my covenant for the day, and my covenant for the night, so that day and night will not be at their appointed times, then my covenant may also be broken with David, my servant, that he shall not have a son to reign on his throne ..." When we allow the devil to make us blind to righteousness and he gives us sight to sin, then God's appointed times for accomplishing His purpose in us are delayed.

And it came to pass, after the year was expired, at the time when kings go forth *to battle*, that David sent Joab, and his servants with him, and all Israel; and they destroyed the children of Ammon, and besieged Rabbah. But David tarried still at Jerusalem.

And it came to pass in an eveningtide, that David arose from off his bed, and walked upon the roof of the king's house: and from the roof he saw a woman washing herself; and the woman *was* very beautiful to look upon.

II Samuel 11:1-2

5

And Nathan said to David, Thou *art* the man. Thus saith the Lord God of Israel, I anointed thee king over Israel, and I delivered thee out of the hand of Saul

II Samuel 12:7

We can find, here, an example of the devil changing the times in the life of David. It was a time of war. It was a time when kings go to battle. It was an opportunity to be victorious again over the enemies of the Promised Land. But the devil caused this time of war to become a time of comfort for David. The devil has a way of using our victories over him to relax us, and that allows the spirit of comfort to come. The timing of the devil and the comfort of David caused him to go outside right at the time when a beautiful woman was bathing just next door. David's look became a lust. David's lust became a sin. And finally, David's sin became a lifestyle. And it took a prophet of God to come to him and tell him, "Thou art the man." By Nathan revealing David's sin to him and the prophetic anointing causing him to repent, it changed the season of sin into a season of repentance and forgiveness.

He who keeps a *royal* command experiences no trouble, for a wise heart knows the proper time and procedure.

For there is a proper time and procedure for every delight, when a man's trouble is heavy upon him.

Ecclesiastes 8:5-6 (NASB)

Has not Jesus been made unto us wisdom **(I Cor 1:30)**? Does not James say, "if any lack wisdom, let him ask of God without wavering" **(Jam 1:5-6)**? Well then we have no excuse. The wisdom of God not only reveals to us the times of God, but also the procedure of what to do in that time. We might all know about the "proper time." The proper time is always the right time. It is the time that God has ordained to accomplish His purpose in our lives.

The Tribe of Issachar

Now these *are* they that came to David to Ziklag, while he yet kept himself close because of Saul the son of Kish: and they *were* among the mighty men, helpers of the war.

They were armed with bows, and could use both the right hand and the left in *hurling* stones and *shooting* arrows out of a bow, *even* of Saul's brethren of Benjamin.

The chief *was* Ahiezer, then Joash, the sons of Shemaah the Gibeathite; and Jeziel, and Pelet, the sons of Azmaveth; and Berachah, and Jehu the Antothite,

And Ismaiah the Gibeonite, a mighty man among the thirty, and over the thirty; and Jeremiah, and Jahaziel, and Johanan, and Josabad the Gederathite,

Eluzai, and Jerimoth, and Bealiah, and Shemariah, and Shephatiah the Haruphite,

Elkanah, and Jesiah, and Azareel, and Joezer, and Jashobeam, the Korhites,

And Joelah, and Zebadiah, the sons of Jeroham of Gedor.

And of the Gadites there separated themselves unto David into the hold to the wilderness men of might, *and* men of war *fit* for the battle, that could handle shield and buckler, whose faces *were like* the faces of lions, and *were* as swift as the roes upon the mountains;

Ezer the first, Obadiah the second, Eliab the third,

Mishmannah the fourth, Jeremiah the fifth,

Attai the sixth, Eliel the seventh,

Johanan the eighth, Elzabad the ninth,

Jeremiah the tenth, Machbanai the eleventh.

These *were* of the sons of Gad, captains of the host: one of the least *was* over a hundred, and the greatest over a thousand.

These *are* they that went over Jordan in the first month, when it had overflown all his banks; and they put to flight all *them* of the valleys, *both* toward the east, and toward the west.

And there came of the children of Benjamin and Judah to the hold unto David.

And David went out to meet them, and answered and said unto them, If ye be come peaceably unto me to help me, mine heart shall be knit unto you: but if *ye be come* to betray me to mine enemies, seeing *there is* no wrong in mine hands, the God of our fathers look *thereon*, and rebuke *it.*

Then the spirit came upon Amasai, *who was* chief of the captains, *and he said*, "Thine *are* we, David, and on thy side, thou son of Jesse: peace, peace *be* unto thee, and peace *be* to thine helpers; for thy God helpeth thee." Then David received them, and made them captains of the band.

And there fell *some* of Manasseh to David, when he came with the Philistines against Saul to battle: but they helped them not: for the lords of the Philistines upon advisement sent him away, saying, He will fall to his master Saul to *the jeopardy of* our heads.

As he went to Ziklag, there fell to him of Manasseh, Adnah, and Jozabad, and Jediael, and Michael, and Jozabad, and Elihu, and Zilthai, captains of the thousands that *were* of Manasseh.

And they helped David against the band *of the rovers*: for they *were* all mighty men of valor, and were captains in the host.

For at *that* time day by day there came to David to help him, until *it was* a great host, like the host of God.

And these *are* the numbers of the bands *that were* ready armed to the war, *and* came to David to Hebron, to turn the kingdom of Saul to him, according to the word of the LORD.

The children of Judah that bare shield and spear *were* six thousand and eight hundred, ready armed to the war.

Of the children of Simeon, mighty men of valor for the war, seven thousand and one hundred.

Of the children of Levi four thousand and six hundred.

And Jehoiada *was* the leader of the Aaronites, and with him *were* three thousand and seven hundred;

And Zadok, a young man mighty of valor, and of his father's house twenty and two captains.

And of the children of Benjamin, the kindred of Saul, three thousand: for hitherto the greatest part of them had kept the ward of the house of Saul.

And of the children of Ephraim twenty thousand and eight hundred, mighty men of valor, famous throughout the house of their fathers.

And of the half tribe of Manasseh eighteen thousand, which were expressed by name, to come and make David king.

And of the children of Issachar, *which were men* that had understanding of the times, to know what Israel ought to do; the heads of them *were* two hundred; and all their brethren *were* at their commandment.

Of Zebulun, such as went forth to battle, expert in war, with all instruments of war, fifty thousand, which could keep rank: *they were* not of double heart.

And of Naphtali a thousand captains, and with them with shield and spear thirty and seven thousand.

9

And of the Danites, expert in war, twenty and eight thousand and six hundred.

And of Asher, such as went forth to battle, expert in war, forty thousand.

And on the other side of Jordan, of the Reubenites, and the Gadites, and of the half tribe of Manasseh, with all manner of instruments of war for the battle, a hundred and twenty thousand.

All these men of war, that could keep rank, came with a perfect heart to Hebron, to make David king over all Israel: and all the rest also of Israel *were* of one heart to make David king.

I Chronicles 12:1-38

I believe that the trait (the trait of understanding the times) that could have come through the generations did not come. Today, God, like in the times of old, is calling out Christians and rallying us together to join local churches, which we sometimes call armies and, many times, the pastors, we call the captains of these armies. Let's see some of the things mentioned in these Scriptures.

In verse one, it says *helpers of war* came to David. It says they were *armed*.

In verse two, it says they were *settled* to use both their right hands and their left.

Verse eight tells us that they were *men of might*. They had *faces like lions*, they were swift, they were roaring at their enemies.

David declares, in verse seventeen, that he received everybody into his army who came peacefully to help. But, he said, "if you have come to betray me to my enemies, then the Heavenly Father will deal with you."

10

Verse twenty-one says, these men came to help David against his enemies — it also said they were *mighty men of valor*, and some of them were known as captains of the host.

Verse twenty-two says that David's *army grew* day-by-day.

Verse twenty-four tells us that 6,800 were added — with shield and spear.

Verse twenty-five says that 7,100 were added — who were *men of valor, mighty men of valor for war.*

Verse twenty-six tells us that of the Levites, there were 4,600.

Verse twenty-seven tells us that 3,700 more joined them.

Verse twenty-eight tells us that 22 captains joined David.

Verse twenty-nine tells us that 3,000 servants joined.

Verse thirty tells us that 20,800 mighty men of valor — and *famous men* joined the army.

Verse thirty-one tells us that 8,000 joined.

Verse thirty-two tells us that *200 men who had understanding of the times* joined David's army.

Verse thirty-three tells us that 50,000 men who were *expert in war* and were *expert in all instruments of war,* men who could keep rank, and men *who were not double-hearted,* joined the army.

Verse thirty-four tells us that 1,000 *captains* and 37,000 men, skilled in shield and spear, joined the army.

Verse thirty-five tells us that 28,600 men, *expert in war*, came to David.

Verse thirty-six tells us that 40,000 men, expert in war, also joined the army.

Verse thirty-seven tells us that 120,000 joined that had all manner of instruments of war for the battle.

Verse thirty-eight says that all these *men of war that could keep rank came with a perfect heart* to David, the captain, and they were all of one heart.

All of them came from different areas of expertise, different camps and from different captains, and yet, could all rally together for the sake of making David king, and winning the battle of their day.

But the interesting thing, which is of great concern, is that, of all the many thousands of people who came to David, only 200 of them had an understanding of the times, and they were from the tribe of Issachar who had knowledge of what Israel should do. Out of all those that gathered together, you might say that the sons of Issachar could be called the "remnant." Is not God calling a remnant out of the Church today (Jer. 23:3)? I say "out of the Church" because many in the Church are not the remnant. They are tares whose planting is of the devil himself, and they refuse to repent and turn fully to God.

I believe that the sons of Issachar were a prophetic people. (I did not say they were prophets, I said they were prophetic.) They were just as prophetic as Ananias, who went to Paul and gave him a word of direction, because he had heard from God about the proper time and procedure for him. It is this anointing that God is blowing upon the Church today. Many believe that the prophetic is just prophesying "thus saith the Lord." But the prophetic calling describes a people who understand the times and seasons in the immediate present, because they know how to hear from God. God is calling a people today who know the times, who know the seasons and who know what to do (procedure), based upon their knowledge of what time and season they are in. Skiing in the summer or swimming in the winter will kill you. You have to find out what season you are in.

Time of Preparation

In order for us to tune our frequency into the "Time Zone" of God — that being the prophetic anointing hovering over the land — I believe there must be a time of preparation. In order for us to be a prepared people, we must prepare ourselves. God is calling a prophetic people, today, who know how to hear from Him, speak the Word of God and do the work of God. These prophetic people will demonstrate the purposes of God for their lives and for their generations. They will place themselves in a position where God's preparational process can begin.

I beseech you therefore, brethren, by the mercies of God, that ye present your bodies a living sacrifice, holy, acceptable unto God, *which is* your reasonable service.

And be not conformed to this world: but be ye transformed by the renewing of your mind, that ye may prove what *is* that good, and acceptable and perfect, will of God.

Romans 12:1-2

The place of sacrifice is at the altar. Those things that God sees in our lives (things which are closest to us) which may give way to stumbling, He wants us to bring to the altar. There are many Issacs that we need to bring to the altar. The place of preparation starts at the altar. Jesus' ministry to the world did not start until he reached thirty years of age. The disciples could not "go into all the world" until they received power from on high on the day of Pentecost.

God sometimes lets us see a glimpse of the finished product, and He uses that to motivate us not to go off course and to persevere in fulfilling the call upon our lives. We know that God used the wilderness to prepare the nation of Israel for the Promised Land. We know that God used Median to prepare Moses to become the great deliverer of the oppressed nation. The wilderness experiences that God desires for us to walk through are times and seasons of preparation.

God's part in the time of preparation is to lead us to that place and cause those events that are ordained by Him to occur. We, then, have a part to play. God has called us to cooperate and co-labor with Him. God will never make us do anything against our own will, and the time of preparation becomes a place where God makes us willing to line up our will with His.

> **And the child Samuel ministered unto the Lord before Eli. And the word of the Lord was precious in those days;** *there was* **no open vision.**
>
> **And it came to pass at that time, when Eli** *was* **laid down in his place, and his eyes began to wax dim,** *that* **he could not see.**
>
>

I Samuel 3:1-2

Here in the Scriptures, we find "that the Word of the Lord was rare in those days" and God, even at that time, was calling forth those that would flow with the prophetic anointing. We find Samuel "ministering unto the Lord." Samuel was placing himself in a position and tuning himself into a certain frequency by preparing his own heart for God to speak. The Old Testament terminology for what Samuel was doing was "seeking His face." We find, over and over, those who God called to "seek His face." Lambs and bulls were still being slaughtered; music at the festivals was still being played; enemies in the Promised Land were still being conquered, but still there was a call to seek His face. When God calls us to seek Him, He wants us to set our heart in expectancy and humility for change to occur. The time of preparation is a place of change.

Maturity

In the womb he took his brother by the heel, And in his maturity he contended with God.

Yes, he wrestled with the angel and prevailed; He wept and sought His favor. He found Him at Bethel, And there He spoke with us.

Hosea 12:3-4 (NASB)

We find that it was "in his [Jacob's] maturity that he contended with God. Yes, he wrestled with the angel and prevailed, he wept and sought His favor." This story tells of Jacob's wrestling all night with the Angel of the Lord. He tells the Angel that he will not let go until a blessing comes. Jacob was crying out for change.

This time of preparation was the place of dislocation. God was taking some things out and putting some things in, and Israel (Jacob's new name) has never walked the same since. The blessing he received was not a new Mercedes Benz or even a fat bank account, but it was a change of his very nature to fulfill the purpose of God. The works of the flesh would now be very foreign to Jacob, for with seeking God with all of his heart, he received the ability and anointing from God to do His will.

The secret to hearing from God is being in the presence of God, and we get there by seeking Him. There are many churches today that God desires for His name to dwell in. Where His name dwells is where His presence is, and where His presence is manifested is where He is speaking. We find, in the Body of Christ today, many churchgoers who cannot hear the Word of the Lord because they are in a cultic place. They are offering their sacrifices (tithes, offerings, time, etc.) in a place where God's name has not been chosen to dwell in.

You can go to these people and tell them that the cloud of the Holy Spirit has moved, and they will say, "the glory of God manifested here years ago, and we have been doing it the same way since." Every place that God's name is not manifested is a cultic place, and the only word you will receive there is, "get out of this place for My presence has left." When God's presence leaves a church, He does not blow a trumpet and sound an alarm about His leaving. Only those that are His (part of the real sheepfold) will know and understand that the cloud of the Lord is moving.

Time of Discernment

In discussing the "Time Zones" of God for the Church corporately and for us as believers individually, we have but only touched the tip of the iceberg. I hear, in my spirit, a trumpet call blowing "discernment, discernment, discernment." There are many within the Church today who have no discernment. They do not study their Bibles — they do not even read their Bibles, for they depend upon man to feed them and, therefore, have no balance for discernment. Everything, and I mean everything, must be judged by the Word of God (the Scriptures). Even when receiving a prophetic word, before you can discern it by your spirit (your recreated human spirit), you had better check out the Word of God, for it is the final authority.

If "a word" is not a word from "the Word," then it is to be utterly rejected. I believe that even after a time of preparation, there has to come a **"time of discernment."** Hear what I say. Discernment will be the one major characteristic of a prophetic people. Those with discernment will not question the voice of God. They will not have to go and get two or three confirmations, for when God speaks, they know it is He speaking. Ask yourself a question: When God speaks to you, do you know it is He speaking? I am not talking about "spiritual guessing," for many in the Body have that gift. I am talking about discernment about the times and seasons of God. The greater our knowledge of the Word of God, the keener our discernment will be.

Time of Fire

God has set and appointed special times and seasons for us (the Church) to walk in, that they might mold us and shape us into that chaste Bride of Christ. Times and seasons of fire have been ordained to walk through. It was this revelation that John the Baptist preached about.

> **And the axe is already laid at the root of the trees; every tree therefore that does not bear good fruit is cut down and thrown into the fire.**

> **As for me, I baptize you with water for repentance, but He who is coming after me is mightier than I, and I am not fit to remove His sandals; He will baptize you with the Holy Spirit and fire.**

> **Matthew 3:10-11 (NASB)**

The "fire" here was not only the tongues of fire on the Day of Pentecost, but the fire that would mature the Church unto perfection. The Holy Spirit reveals this in Acts, chapter fourteen:

> **And after they had preached the gospel to that city and had made many disciples, they returned to Lystra and to Iconium and to Antioch,**

17

strengthening the souls of the disciples, encouraging them to continue in the faith, and *saying,* **"Through many tribulations we must enter the kingdom of God."**

Acts 14:21-22 (NASB)

The degree of the Kingdom established in you is in direct proportion to the tests and trials you go through. There is a difference between "seeing" the Kingdom and "entering" the Kingdom. Jesus told Nicodemus that you must be born again to "see" the Kingdom, but you must be born of the water and the spirit to "enter" in. We know that water is for purifying and cleansing. David knew about the purifying season of God, for he wrote, "how shall a young man cleanse his way, but by taking heed to the Word of God."

The nation of Israel knew well about the time of refining and testing.

And you shall remember all the way which the Lord your God has led you in the wilderness these forty years, that He might humble you, testing you, to know what was in your heart, whether you would keep His commandments or not.

Deuteronomy 8:2 (NASB)

We know that the cloud of God led them by day and the fire of God led them by night.

Chapter II

The Zones of God

In understanding any move of God we have to, first of all, understand the "Time Zones" of God. We have to understand what a Zone is, and what the characteristics of a Zone are. Many Christians say God is doing a new thing in the land, yet they are unable to discern the Time Zone that the Church is in today. With the urgency of this hour, it is imperative that we, the Church, know the present Zone.

What Is a Zone?

Let us take a look at the word, "Zone," first. The word, "Zone," is derived from the Latin word "zona," which means "belt" or "girdle." This word is used to describe an area that is encircled by something else. This area that has been designated is referred to as a "Zone." It is also defined as an area, region or division distinguished from adjacent parts by some distinctive feature or character. Other ways of denoting a Zone are often represented by the words: locale, province, sphere and district. A Zone is actually an area or division that has its own characteristics, mechanism or features that, no matter how similar to other (adjacent) areas that it may appear, is still unique in and of itself.

One popular application of this term is the 15 geographical Zones that exist on the earth. Although very similar in structure, each "Time Zone" differs in one-hour increments as you travel longitudinally to the next Zone. These Zones are defined by "belts," which run north and south on the earth's axis.

Now, let us apply this knowledge to the "Zones of God." God's Zones may include a particular feature or use found in a previous Zone yet, as He moves from Zone to Zone, the present Zone is always unique in and of itself. God, Himself, encircles His own areas and orchestrates His own features or characteristics within these regions and, therefore, owns these Zones Himself. One other definition of the word, "Zone," that may help you visualize God's Zones is that the actual area is a region comprised between definite limits, or a limited area distinguished from those adjacent by some quality or condition. And in the case of God, He sets the limits, and He creates the qualities or conditions.

There is a great need for sound and consistent teaching to take place within the Body of Christ about the new Time Zone of God that we are facing. We have to study the boundaries of this Zone. Many Christians have been in various Zones without even knowing their boundaries. If you don't know the boundaries of your Zone, you will operate inappropriately. You will find yourself operating and acting one Zone for the other. We have to study the width, the breadth, the length and the height of the Zone. We have to determine the beginning of each Zone, the characteristics of that Zone and the end of the Zone. We have to know where the line is drawn between the old Zone and the new one that we are in.

Many believers make great mistakes because of their lack of understanding of the Zone that we are in. If you are not sure of the Zone that you are in, you will operate illegally, never reaching your full potential. It is not surprising that a lot of Christians do not operate to their fullest potentials, because they practice syncretism. They mix the religion, the idea and practices of one Zone for another.

The first sign that will confirm that we are in a new Zone is the blowing of the trumpet of God by the prophets and the apostles. This blowing of the trumpet signifies the ending of one Zone and the beginning of another. So, actually, what we have is the limits or boundaries being defined by the blowing trumpets in the land. It is, therefore, crucial that we acknowledge these boundaries. This acknowledgment will cause an individual to become sensitive toward the current changes being made. But, what has happened is that some people have become so relaxed and content with the previous Zone, they have allowed their spiritual sensory organs to become "dead." Their spiritual antennae have become defective, and they are unable to pick up the new "approaching object" — a new Zone.

The Characteristics of the New Zone

This particular Zone has very unique characteristics about it. One attribute is that the mantle over this present Zone is prophetic. This invisible mantle is like a huge umbrella, tent or a canopy. This covering is airtight and retains everything underneath it. The "air" that circulates under it is prophetic. Now, of course, the "air" is not limited to a select few that are exposed, but to all. The key here is being "exposed."

Here's a great example of this. Suppose you are under a massive-size tent for a campmeeting, and inside this tent, you are grilling some mouth-watering barbecued ribs. Because of the fabric of the tent, the smoke only permeates out of the top of the tent and the smell of the cooking never escape. It remains in the tent. Therefore, the luxury of smelling the ribs can only be enjoyed by those who reside within the parameters of the tent, and those on the outside not only miss out on the awesome smell, but they don't even get to witness the sight of those delicious barbecued ribs. Let's bring it a little closer to home. The aroma (anointing, power, the prophetic mantle) can be experienced only by those who reside within the very limits (boundaries) of the tent (zone).

The great truth is that once you have entered the area designated by the canopy (mantle), you then are entitled to share in that great smell (the prophetic). It's good to know that this new Zone offers an all-inclusive ministry. The prophetic ministry is available for all those who will embrace it. This ministry is not limited to the prophets and the apostles. The prophets and apostles will have a predominant role, but they won't just run the show.

This news is especially good for those who walk in offices other than the prophet. This will allow everyone to be content where God has called them, and cause many to return unto their original calling. These "intruders" who aborted their areas of ministry and invaded others will realize that the prophetic is also available to them, once they embrace it, in the very place they belong, whether that is the office of a prophet or not. In essence, this Time Zone will produce men and women who are not just teachers, but teachers who will flow in the prophetic teaching anointing. The same will apply to the pastors, the evangelists and the apostles. These offices will be prophetic.

Prophets that Are Not Prophetic

The startling thing about this is that there will be prophets during this endtime who will not be prophetic, for the mere fact that they did not embrace the mantle or did not enter the new Zone. A lot of Christians think that simply because they are prophets, that makes them automatically prophetic. No, that is not true. There are still false prophets. False prophets cannot be prophetic. They cannot give the immediate Word of the Lord. They will not be able to give the "Now Word". They will be talking about themselves and giving words from past Time Zones. Just as God is concerned about the prophets and the apostles, God is also concerned about the pastors, teachers and the evangelists. All of the five-fold ministry gifts must embrace this new move of the Spirit of God, within this new Time Zone, in order to be prophetic. As mentioned earlier, prophets will play a major role with respect to this Zone, along with the apostles. They both will be the ones to lead the people to the "tent." They will also be the ones to open the door for the rest to enter.

How Do I Know I Am in This Zone?

Now you might be saying, "Well, since this canopy, tent, or mantle is invisible, how will I know when I have entered?" As we began earlier, I started pointing out characteristics. Besides being prophetic, you will notice that there is a supernatural lubrication that is provided. This lubrication allows you to do certain things, like minister with minimum effort. There will be great ease provided when doing what you are supposed to do within this Zone. Another clue is that there is a common terminology used and shared among the individuals residing within this Zone.

Restoration

As we look back over the past years of the Church, we can see how God has been restoring many things. There were some who received the revelation of baptism by immersion — and they called themselves "Baptists." There were some who received the revelation of justification — and they called themselves "Lutherans." There were some who received the revelation about sanctification and holiness — and they called themselves "Methodists." There were those who got the revelation about the Holy Spirit — and they called themselves "Pentecostals." In the last forty or fifty years, God has given us the revelation about healing, laying on of hands, the gifts of the Spirit, intercessory prayer and the teaching of the Word of God. God has restored to us the anointing of the evangelist and teacher; and we know there were always pastors on the scene.

The three-fold cord of the pastor, teacher and evangelist is now being broken, for now is the time that God is giving us the revelation, and restoring the anointing of the prophet and the apostle back to the Church. God is calling out a prophetic and apostolic people — people who will know the times and the seasons of God; people who will know how to hear from God and understand what to do with what they have heard; people who have become intimate with the living God and who will know how to activate and impart that anointing, that they have received through that intimacy, to others; people who will know how to pluck up those things that have not been planted by God and break down those things that have been set up by the devil; people who will know how to destroy the works of the enemy and overthrow the strategies and devices of principalities and powers. They will be people who know how to build up and bring edification to those around them, and they will know how to plant and cultivate special anointings in the days to come.

The Instrument, the Assignment (Purpose) and the People

There are three important things that every believer must ascertain in order to thoroughly understand the Time Zones of God.

First of all, you must be able to identify and locate the "instrument" for the Zone. It is the appropriate instrument that will allow individuals to operate at an optimal level of efficiency in all that they do. The instrument of a Time Zone is the thing that God has chosen to birth, operate, serve and complete His purpose within the boundaries of that particular Time Zone. The instrument can be an office, an individual, an idea or even a certain strategy — all being able to ensure the completion of God's purpose. Throughout the Bible, we can detect the introduction and usage of many instruments during many Time Zones. In order to secure success within a present Time Zone, we must be sure to be associated with the current instrument of the hour. You must determine what instrument God is using, or intends to use, to pioneer His movement. Again, as we look back over the past years of the Church, we can see how God used certain instruments to pioneer His move. A good example is the great "Healing-Wave Revival" of 1948 and 1949. The Spirit of God created a Zone in which the healing anointing, mantle, covering, umbrella and canopy was the talk of the town. There was an emergence of great healing leaders like Oral Roberts, T.L. Osborn, Kathryn Kuhlman, A.A. Allen and Jack Cole. These individuals were on the healing map.

Every Christian then wanted to become an evangelist, because they were the talk of the town. They were like the most popular ministers in town. They were the ones on the scene. Many believers that were called to various offices abandoned and aborted their callings, offices and church, and wanted to become an evangelist overnight. They immediately fell in love with the office of the evangelist. They no longer enjoyed, cherished and appreciated the office and position which God had called them to function in.

Note very carefully that the instruments for that movement and Zone was the office of the evangelist. For every move of God there is always an instrument that God uses, or will use to pioneer the movement. Note, also, that it was not that God hated or disliked the other offices then, but that the office of the evangelist was used to pioneer the healing-wave anointing. Interestingly, there were those who were called into the pastoral office, the prophetic office, the teaching office and the apostolic office that were also used by God for that Zone. But the instrument that God used to pioneer the move for that Time Zone was the office of the evangelist.

The Word Revival

The same applied to the "Word Revival Wave." In the wave of the Word Revival, the office of the teacher was the instrument that was used to pioneer the move. The other five-fold ministry gifts participated, but the office of the teacher was the key to the opening of the door to the Word

Revival. Everyone, as with the healing move, wanted to become teachers. The office of the teacher was the one on the scene. Teachers were the talk of the town.

Traveling from Zone to Zone

There are three distinct degrees of affect and influence as one travels from Zone to Zone. All three influences promote a change, but the changes promoted differ in severity of reaction. One change promoted is a gradual, moderate change. Then there is an immediate level of change, one that is less gradual and more abrupt. Then there is the third, which calls for an all-out abrupt change. Let us reflect upon these changes, compare them to everyday living and picture them in relationship to God.

In the first context, there are the Time Zones of God that are very like unto the seasons that we experience. Each season, (Spring, Summer, Winter, Fall) is marked by boundaries, dates that signify that one is over and the next begins. But we very well know that this does not necessarily influence the immediate weather that we experience. The change is often gradual and moderate. Many times of late, we are experiencing the "old weather" in the "new Zone," and we tolerate the old being brought into the new, especially if it means beautiful weather. Many times, a summer day in the month of November is very well welcomed. As with God, there were changes that God expected from us, and yet He tolerated gradual and moderate changes from us; for example, the maturing of the Church.

The next, intermediate, change would be less gradual than above and more abrupt. These changes dictate a more ready response. A great example may be that of a city's boundaries or limits. As we travel from one city to another, we are influenced by different rules, regulations, tax structures etc. Oftentimes, operating within the mode of one city within the realm of another would institute certain warnings and maybe even fines.

26

A good example of this can be found within the city limits of New York City. There is a law that if you are operating your windshield wipers, you must also have your headlights on. In every city in New Jersey, this is not a law. Travelling from New Jersey to New York is very simple, but dictates changes that must be adhered to. Now, a New Jersey motorist found not adhering to this law may receive a warning or even a fine. Most times, the fact that he or she is a New Jersey motorist is taken into consideration and influences the penalty. Different from the changes above, there becomes an influence of those in authority within that "Zone," within the limits of that city.

One thing is certain: travelling from one "Zone" to the next causes you to fall under the ordinances of that next "Zone." Although the change is more drastic, more abrupt than the first, it still is somewhat gradual as before. Some slackness, tardiness, slothfulness is tolerated. But here the leniency is up to those in authority (another example is the right turn on red lights allowed in certain states, not in others).

The third and final stage is likened to a "speed zone." This change is least desirable because it "demands" a very abrupt change. It demands extreme reaction, an immediate response. It is apparent that it is illegal to travel across the boundary — the "line of change" — the old way, using the old pattern, the old style. Take, for instance, a road on the highway that has a 55 MPH speed limit and where 65 MPH is allowed on it but it empties into a residential road that has a speed limit of 25 MPH. This point of change is marked with a sign which reads "speed zone." This zone demands immediate response, an abrupt change. Often, police officers will man these locations to enforce this law and usually are quite busy in writing speeding tickets. Why? Because people fail to realize that change is on demand. A response is almost needed "yesterday."

Let's look at this as it refers to the Church. Take a baby Christian who has just newly joined the family of God. There are certain changes that he or she will experience. Through God's sovereign tolerance, many will be allowed to be dropped off gradually — certain habits. Some demand immediate change. But in order to distinguish which need immediate response and which can have a gradual response, you need to hook up with the One in authority, God! It remains a sin for believers to at one time be granted gradual changes in some areas and they create a pattern with this and address every change at hand with the same reaction. No, no, no!! Some things God is telling us to do now! "Change now." "Let go of that old stuff, that old way, that old tool." "This is a new way of Mine, it must be done differently."

As in the examples above, people experience different penalties in traveling from "Zone to Zone" in the same way. Well, there are also "penalties" for the same violations in relationship to God. Not being in tune to the appropriate change that is necessary by the demands dictated by God brings about violations. These violations are observed by those who are infested with traditionalism. This is a result of a person, or group of people, not "reacting" to the change that God had demanded at that time. These people refused to move on in God, and the result is "spiritual lethargy" — acting out of tradition.

Another common violation observed is one's consistent inaccuracy of the things of God. This results from the refusal or inability to keep up with God in the "now," causing a frequent hit-and-miss syndrome by an individual. (See my book, "*Developing Spiritual Accuracy and Pinpointing.*") It is very important to react immediately to what God is demanding. The response dictated this time is of the abrupt nature.

Therefore, as we see the pattern being set above, the neglect of responding in a timely fashion will bring about a much harsher "penalty." These violations today will be marked by gross spiritual atrophy. Individuals behind the times will stick out like a sore thumb. Churches that refuse to change and insist upon traveling into this new "Zone" in the old way will dry up spiritually. These places of worship will appear as valleys of dry bones. Because of the extreme reaction needed on the part of the Body of Christ, it will be obvious, this time, everyone who will not move with God. Traditionalism will be poisonous.

Now that we have seen the repercussions of not moving, what can we do? We, first of all, need to study each Zone and identify the necessary changes and degrees of reaction prompted by each Zone. Once we have done this, we must be obedient and flow with that change that is before us. We must no longer be ready to do things at our own "pace," but we need to hook up with who is in authority, God, and get on His time schedule.

The Club

"Don't be ridiculous!" Saul replied. "How can a kid like you fight with a man like him? You are only a boy and he has been in the army *since* he was a boy!"

But David persisted. "When I am taking care of my father's sheep," he said, "and a lion or a bear comes and grabs a lamb from the flock,

I go after it with a club and take the lamb from its mouth. If it turns on me I catch it by the jaw and club it to death.

I have done this to both lions and bears, and I'll do it to this heathen Philistine too, for he has defied the armies of the living God!

The Lord who saved me from the claws and teeth of the lion and the bear will save me from this Philistine!"

I Samuel 17:33-37 (TLB)

Before David was anointed king of Israel, he was taking care of his father, Jesse's, sheep. The Bible lets us know that, while taking care of his father's sheep, he killed the bear and the lion with the club. Note,

29

carefully, the instrument that was used in killing the bear and the lion. It was the club.

The Stones, the Staff, the Sling

And Saul armed David with his armour, and he put an helmet of brass upon his head; also he armed him with a coat of mail.

And David girded his sword upon his armour, and he assayed to go; for he had not proved *it*. **And David said unto Saul, I cannot go with these; for I have not proved** *them*. **And David put them off him.**

And he took his staff in his hand, and chose him five smooth stones out of the brook, and put them in a shepherd's bag which he had, even in a scrip; and his sling *was* **in his hand: and he drew near to the Philistine.**

I Samuel 17:38-40

When David came before Goliath of Gath, it was a different story. He did not use the club that was successful for him in killing the lions and the bears while he was a shepherd. He realized that the two Zones were different. He knew he was in a new Zone. He knew that the instrument of the club for the old Zone would not be successful for the new Zone. He would have been foolish to use the club again. He discerned the instrument that was needed for the new Zone. He sought out the instrument for that Time Zone. Even though Saul was trying to persuade him to use his instrument of war, David refused. He turned down Saul's offer.

David was able to ascertain the instrument that God wanted him to use for that Time Zone. David wanted the instrument for the hour. He found it in the "five stones," the "staff" and the "sling." I believe that this was not the first time that David was using the stones, shepherd's staff and the sling. As a shepherd boy, he must have used them before. He was skillful in using these instruments, yet he never used it against the lions and bears.

He, instead, used the club. If he had used the stones, the staff and the sling against the lions and bears, he would not have been successful, because he would have been using the wrong instrument for that Zone.

But against Goliath, it was the hour of the stones, staff and sling, not the instruments of war offered to him by King Saul, nor his club (the instrument of the old Zone). It was a new Time Zone, and a new instrument of operation was needed and demanded.

Songs of Victory and Praise

Using the new and correct instrument for a movement and a Time Zone will launch you into the path that God wants you to follow.

And it came to pass as they came, when David was returned from the slaughter of the Philistine, that the women came out of all cities of Israel, singing and dancing to meet king Saul, with tabrets, with joy, and with instruments of music.

And the women answered *one another* **as they played, and said, Saul hath slain his thousands, and David his ten thousands.**

And Saul was very wroth, and the saying displeased him; and he said, They have ascribed unto David ten thousands, and to me they have ascribed *but* **thousands: and** *what* **can he have more but the kingdom?**

I Samuel 18:6-8

David's instrument of stones, staff and sling brought Goliath flat on his face. The aggressor of that time was defeated by the instrument ordained for that Time Zone, not the instrument of the old Zone. Goliath of Gath was a type of enemy then, and is a type of enemy today. All it took was the proper instrument.

31

There was a new move in the land after the defeat of Goliath. Joy was restored back to Israel. Israel became a formidable opponent to be reckoned with. There was a fresh revival within the land. There emerged a new people, with a fresh desire and zeal. They saw the faithfulness of God in operation. All it took was the use of the proper instrument for the correct Time Zone. David's ministry was heralded all throughout the land. He was the talk of the town. He became popular overnight. He caught the attention of Israel. All just because he understood the Time Zones of God, he studied his boundary and understood the instrument for that Zone. He obeyed God.

The Draft Is Out, the Line is Drawn in the Sand

God is calling for a people who will be able to understand the Time Zone that the Church is in today — a people that will vigorously study, understand and interpret the extent, width, breadth and height of the boundary, and be able to locate the instrument for the Zone.

We still have men that are using the club against the Goliath of our day, instead of the stones, the staff and the sling. It is imperative that the Church identify and cherish the instrument of this present move of the Spirit of God. The Church must discern the instrument of the hour. The Body of Christ has been using outdated instruments for a long time. One of the reasons that the Church has not experienced the great exploits, revival and outpouring promised by God as we should, is because we are still in the business of using old tools and outdated instruments. Simply because it worked well once for us in one Zone, we immediately think that it will work the same way within another Zone.

Just like the instrument of the club, after the completion of the task of killing Goliath, David's instrument of stones, staff and sling became outdated. They had completed their job. They were no longer useful. They were now useless. Any attempt to use them again in another Zone would not produce lubrication and the flow for that Zone. David's instrument for his future wars and when he became a king was no longer stones, staves or slings, nor was it a club. He used other instruments meant for those Time Zones.

There are many leaders and ministers still using the old instrument of ideas, tactics and strategies of one Time Zone for the other. The ideas, tactics and strategies may have been successful while they were used for that Time Zone, but that does not mean that they will be successful in this new Time Zone of God. They think, because they were successful in building great churches and projects with the old ideas, tactics and strategies, that they can use them for this new Zone. With every Zone comes new instruments. When you find that you are not successful, dried up, rigid and starchy, and cannot flow like you used to, what you need to do is to check the instrument that you are using. Is it the old or the new instrument? The old will be rusty and void of lubrication.

The problem is this: the old instrument of ideas, tactics and strategies may yield some little dividends, but it will not be to the full propensity that God intends. Our leaders, ministers and the entire Body of Christ must check what instrument we are using. Is it the outdated instrument or the new, updated instrument? If you discover that you are still using an old instrument of ideas, tactics, strategies or whatever, let it go so that God, in this new Time Zone, will give to you a new instrument meant for the new move.

What Instruments Are You Wearing?

And Saul armed David with his armour, and he put an helmet of brass upon his head; also he armed him with a coat of mail.

33

And David girded his sword upon his armour, and he assayed to go; for he had not proved *it*. **And David said unto Saul, I cannot go with these; for I have not proved** *them*. **And David put them off him.**

I Samuel 17:38-39

Saul's instrument was an instrument for the old movement. Since Saul was rejected by God, his instrument of war was outdated. The wearing of that instrument would bring failure and defeat. Even though Saul did not realize it, David's wearing of his war instruments would have brought defeat. David refused to use Saul's outdated instrument. He preferred the instrument which came from the presence of God. Most Christians are still wearing strange instruments of war. Saul's instrument did not fit David. David was not comfortable with it. He was not used to it. Why? Because it was outdated.

When an instrument is outdated and meant for an old movement its use becomes uncomfortable. It becomes rusty. The instrument of an old movement and Zone will not fit the people of a new Time Zone. Its operation will be difficult. David opted for what he was comfortable with. He opted for something new and fresh.

Let's look at the life and ministry of Samson. His life and ministry will bring clarity and shed light on the issue of the instrument.

And the woman bare a son, and called his name Samson: and the child grew, and the Lord blessed him.

And the Spirit of the Lord began to move him at *times* **in the camp of Dan between Zorah and Eshtaol.**

Judges 13:24-25

The key word, here, that I want you to note is the word, "times." The Spirit of God at "times" would move on Samson. In other words, at

certain Time Zones, the Spirit of God would move on him in the camp of
Dan between Zorah and Eshtaol. Samson experienced the different moving
of the Spirit of God upon his life within different Time Zones. The
instrument of each of these moves, interestingly, were different.

The Zone of Timnath

**But his father and his mother knew not that it *was* of the Lord, that he
sought an occasion against the Philistines: for at that time the Philistines had
dominion over Israel.**

**Then went Samson down, and his father and his mother, to Timnath, and
came to the vineyards of Timnath: and, behold, a young lion roared against
him.**

**And the spirit of the Lord came mightily upon him, and he rent him as he
would have rent a kid, and *he had* nothing in his hand: but he told not his
father or his mother what he had done.**

Judges 14:4-6

The Spirit of God moved in this very particular time on the life of
Samson "by renting him as he would have rent a kid and he had nothing
in his hand." If there was nothing in his hand, that means he killed the
lion with his bare hands. He only could do this because the Spirit of the
Lord was mightily upon him. So the instrument that was used in this Zone
was his "bare hands."

The Riddle

**And Samson said unto them, I will now put forth a riddle unto you: if ye
can certainly declare it me within the seven days of the feast, and find *it*
out, then I will give you thirty sheets and thirty change of garments:**

But if yet cannot declare *it* me, then shall ye give me thirty sheets and thirty change of garments. And they said unto him, Put forth thy riddle, that we may hear it.

And he said unto them, Out of the eater came forth meat, and out of the strong came forth sweetness. And they could not in three days expound the riddle.

And it came to pass on the seventh day, that they said unto Samson's wife, Entice thy husband, that he may declare unto us the riddle, lest we burn thee and thy father's house with fire: have ye called us to take that we have? *is it*, not *so*?

And Samson's wife wept before him, and said, Thou dost but hate me, and lovest me not: thou has put forth a riddle unto the children of my people, and hast not told *it* me. And he said unto her, Behold, I have not told *it* my father nor my mother, and shall I tell *it* thee?

And she wept before him the seven days, while their feast lasted: and it came to pass on the seventh day, that he told her, because she lay sore upon him: and she told the riddle to the children of her people.

And the men of the city said unto him on the seventh day before the sun went down, What *is* sweeter than honey? and what *is* stronger than a lion? And he said unto them, If ye had not plowed with my heifer, ye had not found out my riddle.

And the spirit of the Lord came upon him, and he went down to Ashkelon, and slew thirty men of them, and took their spoil, and gave change of garments unto them which expounded the riddle. And his anger was kindled, and he went up to his father's house.

Judges 14:12-19

Here was a different instrument that Samson used to cause the move of the Spirit of God. Samson used a riddle to cause the movement of God. Samson gave a riddle with a promise to reward anyone who interpreted the meaning of the riddle. After the riddle was interpreted, the Bible says that "the Spirit of the Lord came upon him, and he went to Ashkelon, and slew thirty men of them and took their spoil, and gave change of garments unto them which expounded the riddle."

The New Jaw Bone of an Ass

Then three thousand men of Judah went to the top of the rock Etam, and said to Samson, Knowest thou not that the Philistines *are* rulers over us? what *is* this *that* thou hast done unto us? And he said unto them, As they did unto me, so have I done unto them.

And they said unto him, We are come down to bind thee, that we may deliver thee into the hand of the Philistines. And Samson said unto them, Swear unto me, that ye will not fall upon me yourselves.

And they spake unto him, saying, No; but we will bind thee fast, and deliver thee into their hand: but surely we will not kill thee. And they bound him with two new cords, and brought him up from the rock.

And when he came unto Lehi, the Philistines shouted against him: and the spirit of the Lord came mightily upon him, and the cords that *were* upon his arms became as flax that was burnt with fire, and his bands loosed from off his hands.

And he found a new jawbone of an ass, and put forth his hand, and took it, and slew a thousand men therewith.

And Samson said, With the jawbone of an ass, heaps upon heaps, with the jaw of an ass have I slain a thousand men.

And it came to pass, when he had made an end of speaking, that he cast away the jawbone out of his hand, and called that place Ramath-lehi.

Judges 15:11-17

Again, the instrument here is different. In this Time Zone, Samson was able to slay the Philistine with the help of a "new jaw bone of an ass."

When the move was completed, Samson threw away the "new jaw bone." It was no longer "new." It was now "old." This is the mistake a lot of leaders and Christians make. They take one move and instrument from one Zone to the other. They transfer an old "jaw bone" to a new Zone. A new Zone demanded a "new jaw bone."

Samson did the right thing. He did not say because he was successful in killing the Philistines with the "new jaw bone," that he should continually use the "jaw bone" for other moves. The Church must learn from the life of Samson.

If this had taken place in this present day, there would be ministers and leaders that would obtain a patent law and a trademark for the usage of the "jaw bone." They would want exclusive rights to the usage of the "jaw bone." They would not want any other person, church or ministry to use the "jaw bone." They would go to Washington, D.C. to register the "jaw bone" under their names and their ministries. You see, what they fail to realize is that the "jaw bone" is no longer new. It is no longer fresh. It has completed its ordained function and purpose. Once its function was completed, the "jaw bone" became old, rusty and outdated. Samson had to immediately throw it away. Why? Because he knew that the instrument was now outdated.

Then Samson said,

"With a donkey's jawbone I have made donkeys of them. With donkey's jawbone I have killed a thousand men."

When he finished speaking, he threw away the jawbone; and the place was called Ramath-lehi.

Judges 15:16-17 (NIV)

Even though Samson was joyous over the victory and the success of the function of the "new jaw bone," he had to throw it away because it was no longer useful. It was now useless. Its purpose and function had been completed. It was now time to move to another Time Zone, with a different instrument, and a different function and purpose. Sometimes we can be deceived into using the same instrument over and over again, without taking the time to discern if the instrument, idea, tactic or strategy is old and outdated. Simply because that idea, tactic or strategy still brings money does not make it new. It can bring in money and, yet, be old and outdated.

I believe that if Samson had used the "new jaw bone of an ass" for another Zone and against another group of people, he would still have been able to kill some of the Philistines. But it would not be a great amount, like he did the very first time when the "jaw bone" was fresh from the manufacturer (God). Samson would not be operating at his optimum or maximum potential. He would be operating at his minimum. God wants the Church to operate at Her optimum and not at Her minimum. In order to be at our optimum and maximum level of potential, we must make sure that our instruments are fresh and new from the manufacturer. The "jaw bone" was successful because it was "new" and not old.

This applies to the Church. Today, if we are still using any form of a "jaw bone" which seems to be new and yet old, we must immediately throw it away and give room for God to give us the new instrument meant for this Time Zone.

Your jaw bone can be a beautiful idea, vision, dream or even strategy to do a thing that God might have given to you sometime ago. While it was given to you, it was very successful, but now you can see how the degree of success has diminished. There is no lubrication left. You are now doing or operating it by your might and strength. It is no longer

100% God in charge. It is 40% God in charge and 60% percent your idea and effort in charge. It no longer produces the 100-fold return. That idea or strategy needs an examination. Examine to see if God still wants you to use that instrument.

What Will Happen When I Let Go?

Many ministers wonder what will happen to them and their ministries if they let go of the instrument, idea, or strategy that had once made them and their ministries successful and famous. Well, let me tell you what will happen. You will not lose a thing. Instead, God will replace that idea, instrument or tactic with a new one. The one you once had is old and outdated. All God wants to do is to help you replace your old idea, vision, dream, tactic or strategy with a new one straight from heaven, that is not void of lubrication. The danger of not opting for a change will be that you and your ministry will always operate at the minimum level. You will never come to the point of your full potential. You can attend all the seminars, conferences and camp meetings, but when everything is said and done, you and your church are back to their old state. We must let go of the old for the new. We must kill the spirit of fear, laziness and complacency that might want to prevent us from opting for the new instrument.

Please make sure that you note very carefully that Samson did not take one move of God from one Time Zone to another. He did not take the equipment, tool, instrument or idea that was responsible for one movement to the other.

For every move, God had fresh equipment, ways and tools to bring down His glory, power, and anointing. That is why it is very important for the Church to understand the timing of God, so that they will not carryover one tool, way or equipment from one move or Time Zone, to another.

The Launching-Out Time

After these things Jesus walked in Galilee: for he would not walk in Jewry: because the Jews sought to kill him.

Now the Jews' feast of tabernacles was at hand.

His brethren therefore said unto him, Depart hence, and go into Judaea, that thy disciples also may see the works that thou doest.

For *there is* no man *that* doeth anything in secret, and he himself seeketh to be known openly. If thou do these things, show thyself to the world.

For neither did his brethren believe in him.

Then Jesus said unto them, My time is not yet come: but your time is alway ready.

The world cannot hate you; but me it hateth, because I testify of it, that the works thereof are evil.

John 7:1-7

Jesus wanted to launch out into the ministry at the proper time. He did not want to be an illegal minister. You are illegal when you don't go through the right door, way or channel. When you go through the window or by the shortcut, you will find yourself operating illegally. Jesus knew and understood the time for everything.

You can do a thing that is absolutely right, but because you did it at the wrong time, it becomes wrong.

When you don't find the purpose for time, you will abuse it. Time has a purpose. God might give you a program or a project to accomplish for Him, during a specific time span, and after that time span that program is supposed to be over, unless God decides to extend it.

41

Illegal Ministers

There are many individuals who say that God has called them into the ministry and, because of this, they jump into the ministry without knowing and understanding the time and the timing period that God wanted them to be in the ministry. As a result of this, the Church has produced illegal ministers within the ministry. The danger of this is these illegal ministers will begin to produce illegal and illegitimate babies as congregation members. These babies will then have the genes and the chromosomes of their fathers. Since God's approval and permission is not stamped on them, they will then have to anoint themselves, because God will not anoint what He has not approved.

> **Verily, verily, I say unto you, He that entereth not by the door into the sheepfold, but climbeth up some other way, the same is a thief and a robber.**
>
> **But he that entereth in by the door is the shepherd of the sheep.**
>
> **To him the porter openeth; and the sheep hear his voice: and he calleth his own sheep by name, and leadeth them out.**
>
> **And when he putteth forth his own sheep, he goeth before them, and the sheep follow him: for they know his voice.**
>
> **And a stranger will they not follow, but will flee from him: for they know not the voice of strangers.**
>
> **John 10:1-5**

The Bible says, if you don't come through the door, you are a "thief" and a "robber." That means you are illegal. You are regarded as a "stranger," and your voice will not be heard or adhered to by your flock.

No matter how good, correct and genuine your message may be, if you are a stranger, nobody will want to listen to what you have to say. A lot of ministers wonder why their ministries are not prospering as God had promised. They fail to understand that they have missed the timing of God.

You can actually be carrying out a vision that is meant for a particular Time Zone during another Time Zone, and you might wonder why God is not prospering that vision. It is because it does not belong to that Time Zone. What you need to do is to determine what God wants you to do during this Time Zone and, as you begin to remain obedient, He will begin to tell you about the vision for the other Time Zones.

You see, to be obedient is to do what God wants, when he wants it, where he wants it, how he wants it, and then to STOP. Anything more is being disobedient.

The Assignments and the Purpose

The second thing to know about the Time Zone of God is the assignment for that Zone. Every Zone has its own assignment. The assignment could be both individually and corporately — we must not fulfill an assignment of one Zone for the other. We must find the assignment for this Time Zone and serve it. Knowing the assignment of a Time Zone will help to determine and decide the boundary for that Zone. The assignment of a Zone is an extension of the boundary of that Zone.

We have men and women who claim God called them into the ministry; yet they have no assignment and purpose. They cannot tell you the assignment they are assigned to. They cannot pinpoint what God exactly wants them to do. Yet they say God has called them.

There are many ministers that are operating outside of their boundaries because they do not know their assignment. When you don't know your assignment or purpose, you will operate outside of your boundaries. When you don't know your boundaries, you will be stepping on someone else's boundaries. You will find yourself doing things that God did not call you to do.

And they arose early: and it came to pass about the spring of the day, that Samuel called Saul to the top of the house, saying, Up, that I may send thee away. And Saul arose, and they went out both of them, he and Samuel, abroad.

***And** as they were going down to the end of the city, Samuel said to Saul, bid the servant pass on before us, (and he passed on) but stand thou still a while, that I may show thee the word of God.*

I Samuel 9:26-27

Then Samuel took a vial of oil, and poured *it* upon his head, and kissed him, and said, *Is it* not because the Lord hath anointed thee *to be* captain over his inheritance?

When thou art departed from me today, then thou shalt find two men by Rachel's sepulchre in the border of Benjamin at Zelzah; and they will say unto thee, The asses which thou wentest to seek are found: and, lo, thy father hath left the care of the asses, and sorroweth for you, saying, What shall I do for my son?

Then shalt thou go on forward from thence, and thou shalt come to the plain of Tabor, and there shall meet thee three men going up to God to Bethel, one carrying three kids, and another carrying three loaves of bread, and another carrying a bottle of wine:

And they will salute thee, and give thee two *loaves* of bread; which thou shalt receive of their hands.

After that thou shalt come to the hill of God, where *is* the garrison of the Philistines: and it shall come to pass; when thou art come thither to the city, that thou shalt meet a company of prophets coming down from the high place with a psaltery, and a tabret, and a pipe, and a harp, before them; and they shall prophesy:

And the spirit of the Lord will come upon thee, and thou shalt prophesy with them, and shalt be turned into another man.

And let it be, when these signs are come unto thee, *that* thou do as occasion serve thee; for God *is* with thee.

And thou shalt go down before me to Gilgal; and behold, I will come down unto thee, to offer burnt offerings, *and* to sacrifice sacrifices of peace offerings: seven days shalt thou tarry, till I come to thee, and show thee what thou shalt do.

I Samuel 10:1-8

Don't you know that every time a prophet went to anoint a person for a particular office in Israel, he went with anointing oil and with an assignment or a purpose. The assignment and purpose is given after the anointing for that office or position is completed. There is always an assignment or purpose. Look at the various assignments given by the Lord through the prophet Samuel to Saul after he was anointed. Samuel told Saul the purpose of his being anointed, "Is it not because the Lord hath anointed thee to be captain over his inheritance?"

And the Lord said unto him, Go, return on thy way to the wilderness of Damascus: and when thou comest, anoint Hazael *to be* King over Syria:

And Jehu the son of Nimshi shalt thou anoint *to be* king over Israel: and Elisha the son of Shaphat of Abel-meholah shalt thou anoint *to be* prophet in thy room.

And it shall come to pass, *that* **him that escapeth the sword of Hazael shall Jehu slay: and him that escapeth from the sword of Jehu shall Elisha slay.**

I Kings 19:15-17

Do you see the purpose for the anointing of Hazael, Jehu and Elisha in these Scriptures. Hazael was to be anointed as king in place of Benhadad, and the purpose of his anointing was for him to destroy the house of Benhadad, who was not walking in line with God. Jehu was to be anointed as king to replace Ahab, and the purpose of his anointing was for Jehu to destroy all of the house of Ahab. Elisha was to be anointed in Elijah's stead.

And Elisha came to Damascus; and Benhadad the king of Syria was sick; and it was told him, saying, The man of God is come hither.

And the king said unto Hazael, Take a present in thine hand, and go, meet the man of God, and inquire of the Lord by him, saying, Shall I recover of this disease?

So Hazael went to meet him, and took a present with him, even of every good thing of Damascus, forty camels' burden, and came and stood before him, and said, Thy son Benhadad king of Syria hath sent me to thee, saying, Shall I recover of this disease?

And Elisha said unto him, Go, say unto him, Thou mayest certainly recover: howbeit the Lord hath shown me that he shall surely die.

And he settled his countenance steadfastly, until he was ashamed: and the man of God wept.

And Hazael said, Why weepeth my lord? And he answered, Because I know the evil that thou wilt do unto the children of Israel: their strong holds wilt thou set on fire, and their young men wilt thou slay with the sword, and wilt dash their children, and rip up their women with child.

And Hazael said, But what *is* thy servant a dog, that he should do this great thing? And Elisha answered, the Lord hath shown me that thou *shalt be* king over Syria.

So he departed from Elisha, and came to his master; who said to him, What said Elisha to thee? And he answered, He told me *that* thou shouldest surely recover.

And it came to pass on the morrow, that he took a thick cloth, and dipped *it* in water, and spread *it* on his face, so that he died: and Hazael reigned in his stead.

II Kings 8:7-15

And Elisha the prophet called one of the children of the prophets, and said unto him, Gird up thy loins, and take this box of oil in thine hand, and go to Ramoth-gilead:

And when thou comest thither, look out there Jehu the son of Jehoshaphat the son of Nimshi, and go in, and make him arise up from among his brethren, and carry him to an inner chamber;

Then take the box of oil, and pour *it* on his head, and say, Thus saith the Lord, I have anointed thee king over Israel. Then open the door, and flee, and tarry not.

So the young man, *even* the young man the prophet, went to Ramoth-gilead.

And when he came, behold, the captains of the host *were* sitting; and he said, I have an errand to thee, O captain. And Jehu said, Unto which of all us? And he said, To Thee, O captain.

And he arose, and went into the house; and he poured the oil on his head, and said unto him, Thus saith the Lord God of Israel, I have anointed thee king over the people of the Lord, *even* over Israel.

And thou shalt smite the house of Ahab thy master, that I may avenge the blood of my servants the prophets, and the blood of all the servants of the Lord, at the hand of Jezebel.

For the whole house of Ahab shall perish: and I will cut off from Ahab him that pisseth against the wall, and him that is shut up and left in Israel:

And I will make the house of Ahab like the house of Jeroboam the son of Nebat, and like the house of Baasha the son of Ahijah:

And the dogs shall eat Jezebel in the portion of Jezreel, and *there shall be none to bury her.* And he opened the door and fled.

And it come to pass, when Joram saw Jehu, that he said, *is it* peace, Jehu? And he answered, What peace, so long as the whoredoms of thy mother Jezebel and her witchcrafts *are so* many?

And Joram turned his hands, and fled, and said to Ahaziah, *There is* treachery, O Ahaziah.

And Jehu drew a bow with his full strength, and smote Jehoram between his arms, and the arrow went out at his heart, and he sunk down in his chariot.

Then said *Jehu* to Bidkar his captain, Take up *and* cast him in the portion of the field of Naboth the Jezreelite: for remember how that, when I and thou rode together after Ahab his father, the Lord laid this burden upon him;

Surely I have seen yesterday the blood of Naboth, and the blood of his sons, saith the Lord; and I will requite thee in this plat, saith the Lord. Now therefore take *and* cast him into the plat *of ground,* according to the word of the Lord.

But when Ahaziah the king of Judah saw *this,* he fled by the way of the garden house. And Jehu followed after him, and said, Smite him also in the chariot. *And they did so* at the going up to Gur, which *is* by Ibleam. And he fled to Megiddo, and died there.

48

And his servants carried him in a chariot to Jerusalem, and buried him in his sepulchre with his fathers in the city of David.

II Kings 9:1-10,22-28

We see here, all of the assignments and purposes for Jehu's and Hazael's anointing being accomplished. The Church must ascertain the assignment and the purposes of God for this new Time Zone.

The third key characteristic of a Time Zone is the people who are associated with this Zone. These people who embrace the very move of God within that particular Time Zone, through association, begin to develop common characteristics themselves. One of these characteristics that makes these people unique in and of themselves is the development of a kindred spirit.

But I hope *and* trust in the Lord Jesus soon to send Timothy to you, so that I may also be encouraged *and* cheered by learning news of you.

For I have no one like him — no one of so kindred a spirit — who will be so genuinely interested in your welfare *and* devoted to your interests.

Philippians 2:19-20 (AMP)

Once you have become a part of this kindred spirit, you become able to detect those of like spirit through messages, tapes and books. As an individual makes him or herself known in what he or she thinks and believes, your spirit man leaps inside because a connection has been made. The spirits of the individuals join as two gigantic magnets. Inside, your spirit leaps as John the Baptist did when his spirit got hooked up with Jesus' while they were yet still in their mothers' wombs.

And it occurred that when Elizabeth heard Mary's greeting, the baby leaped in her womb; and Elizabeth was filled with *and* controlled by the Holy Spirit.

Luke 1:41 (AMP)

Another quality of these people is the common terminology developed and shared among each other. Subconsciously, a fresh new system of speech arises. This group with a kindred spirit begin to share certain words to express their thoughts, through teachings and preaching. This new common vocabulary begins to replace that of the previous Time Zone. Although the words are still from the English language, meanings have changed and are easily accepted and understood by those present in the current Zone.

Even though there are many other characteristics of these people, this gives an idea of how this group may be identified and subsequently joined, if desired. After a while, an individual is able to detect these people as if they all were arrayed in the brightest pastel colors possible. This is not necessary, because the radar of a keen, developed spirit is sufficient.

Chapter III

The Prophetic Sound

And the Lord spake unto Moses, saying,

Speak unto the children of Israel, saying, In the seventh month, in the first *day* of the month, shall ye have a sabbath, a memorial of blowing of trumpets, an holy convocation.

Ye shall do no servile work *therein*: but ye shall offer an offering made by fire unto the Lord.

Leviticus 23:23-25

And the Lord spake unto Moses, saying,

Make thee two trumpets of silver; of a whole piece shalt thou make them: that thou mayest use them for the calling of the assembly, and for the journeying of the camps. And when they shall blow them, all the assembly shall assemble themselves to thee at the door of the tabernacle of the congregation.

And if they blow *but* with one *trumpet*, then the princes, *which are* heads of the thousands of Israel, shall gather themselves unto thee.

When ye blow an alarm, then the camps that lie on the east parts shall go forward.

When ye blow an alarm the second time, then the camps that lie on the south side shall take their journey: they shall blow an alarm for their journeys.

But when the congregation is to be gathered together, ye shall blow, but ye shall not sound an alarm.

And the sons of Aaron, the priest, shall blow with the trumpets; and they shall be to you for an ordinance for ever throughout your generations.

And if ye go to war in your land against the enemy that oppresseth you, then ye shall blow an alarm with the trumpets; and ye shall be remembered before the Lord your God, and ye shall be saved from your enemies.

Also in the day of your gladness, and in your solemn days, and in the beginnings of your months, ye shall blow with the trumpets over your burnt offerings, and over the sacrifices of your peace offerings; that they may be to you for a memorial before your God: I *am* the Lord your God.

Numbers 10:1-10

And in the seventh month, on the first *day* of the month, ye shall have an holy convocation; ye shall do no servile work: it is a day of blowing the trumpets unto you.

And ye shall offer a burnt offering for a sweet savour unto the Lord; one young bullock, one ram, *and* seven lambs of the first year without blemish.

And their meat offering *shall be of* flour mingled with oil, three tenth deals for a bullock, *and* two tenth deals for a ram,

And one tenth deal for one lamb, throughout the seven lambs:

And one kid of the goats *for* a sin offering, to make an atonement for you:

Beside the burnt offering of the month, and his meat offering, and the daily burnt offering, and his meat offering, and their drink offerings, according unto their manner, for a sweet savour, a sacrifice made by fire unto the Lord.

Numbers 29:1-6

Two trumpets were always used in the Old Testament. These trumpets were described in the book of Numbers: "make thee two trumpets of silver; of a whole piece shalt thou make them: that thou mayest use them for the calling of the assembly, and for the journeyings of the camps." In later years, ram's horns were used, called "shopars."

The purpose of these two trumpets were to proclaim and announce. The people knew how to interpret and how to respond. They knew whether the trumpets were calling them to worship, to walk or to war. They also knew which tribe was being called. They responded to the trumpets as a soldier would react to a call.

Trumpets have discernable calls. They produce sound. They are readily understood by those who will listen. They are clarion calls which demand immediate obedience.

And even things without life giving sound, whether pipe or harp, except they give a distinction in the sounds, how shall it be known what is piped or harped?

For if the trumpet give an uncertain sound, who shall prepare himself to the battle?

So likewise ye, except ye utter by the tongue words easy to be understood, how shall it be known what is spoken? for ye shall speak into the air.

There are, it may be, so many kinds of voices in the world, and none of them *is* without signification.

Therefore if I know not the meaning of the voice, I shall be unto him that speaketh a barbarian, and he that speaketh *shall be* a barbarian unto me.

I Corinthians 14:7-11

Trumpets are heralds. They make declarations, but not of themselves. They require living men with breath in their lungs to take up the trumpets and to blow. Having become living people through the work of the cross, having separated ourselves unto the work of the Lord, and having been filled with the fullness of His Spirit, we can count ourselves qualified to hear and echo the prophetic sound if we believe.

The world surely needs someone to give it direction, for it is bewildered and hopelessly lost. Who is this someone? You and I!

Many times, the words "sound" and "noise" are used interchangeably, while in all actuality they are very different. While they are both heard by the human ears, they are almost opposites of each other.

One dictionary defines noise as **"unwanted sound."** I would like to differentiate the two by saying, a thing heard, that is recognizable and interpretable, is a "sound," while a thing heard that is not recognizable or interpretable is a "noise."

A Child's Cry

Let us take, for example, a mother of an infant, who is in the kitchen busily washing dishes, when all of a sudden she hears the cries of her little one. Immediately, the mother is able to not only recognize, but also interpret, what "sound" is emulating from her child's vocal chords. One familiar sound instructs her to grab a bottle because it is feeding time. Another sound alarms her that there is danger lurking nearby the infant. A third, yet distinct, sound informs the mother that the child desires attention, namely in the form of a hug upon the mother's breast. There is the dreadful sound of the infant having some form of extreme difficulty, which always dictates fear upon the mother. While there are yet more sounds that this one infant can make, each being as distinct as the next, there is one thing in common — they all **dictate a reaction** of some sort. Now, each reaction that the mother chooses may vary, but the key is, she is reacting to something she heard that is recognizable and interpretable, a "sound." Something heard by this same mother of another infant would be unrecognizable and uninterpretable, and probably would not dictate a reaction. This would be a "noise" of another child.

A Car Alarm

Another example would be that of a car alarm. Suppose you had an alarm in your new vehicle, say, a 1993 Mercedes. The activating of your alarm would "sound" a moment of urgency. That all-familiar "sound" would facilitate a reaction from you, unless you live in a congested city area. Each time your alarm were to go off, you would be prompted to inspect its condition or even if it is physically present where you left it. Why? Because you recognize your own alarm's "sound" and you interpret the meaning of its screeching. You can interpret the language that only your alarm can speak and you, of course, react! Now, if another car's alarm is activated, it sends forth a "noise" in your ears, an unwanted sound. Now get this: at the same moment that this may be "noise" in your ears, simultaneously it can be a "sound" in another's ears. So it depends upon who recognizes that which is being heard and who can interpret what's being heard.

By now you are asking, "What does this have to do with anything spiritual?" A lot! There is a lot of forecasting going on within the Body of Christ these days, about trumpets being blown in the land by certain of God's people. This is very much the case. Unfortunately, this creates three distinct groups of individuals, when considering the relationship of the trumpets being blown and the people.

One group, which deserves very little time in describing them, consists of individuals that just don't hear the blowing of the trumpets. They need help indeed! The remaining two groups need differentiating, and then you will see the tie-in with the above examples.

The second group of individuals hear "something" and they, at times, go as far as recognizing what they heard as a trumpet being blown in the land. The problem is they cannot interpret the meaning. They confess that the trumpets are being blown, but they remain just spiritual announcers, announcing and heralding the event but never partaking in the actual event because they lack an interpretation.

As we observed the trend set above, it is the combination of the recognition and, more importantly, the interpretation of what is heard that will promote a what? A reaction! Because this group is without an understanding, without interpretation, they do not react. Remember the school of the prophets at the time of transference of Elijah's spirit to Elisha? They heard something! But, because they were unable to interpret what they had heard, they did not react. The tragic result was that they remained as spectators.

The Body of Christ will be amassed with spiritual spectators in the new move of the Spirit of God. Many will hear something but, without a proper interpretation, they have heard nothing but a "noise." As we have discovered earlier, it is not the "noises" that generate reactions.

Now, for the third group. This group has the ability to recognize the blowing of the trumpets. More than that, they are able to interpret that which they hear. The blowing becomes a "sound" within their ears. Their confession is that they can hear the "sound" of the trumpet! Their famous question to everyone is, "Can't you hear the 'sound'"? Remember, the trumpet is actually God's prophetic voice speaking. Therefore, to have no reaction to the blowing of the trumpet is to not react to what God is saying — that's very dangerous.

The sounding of the trumpet is a type of God's prophetic voice proclaiming the Word of the Lord. The Body of Christ must have a clear prophetic ear to hear it.

Purposes for the Blowing of the Trumpet

Some of the purposes for which the trumpets were used are as follows:

And when they shall blow with them, all the assembly shall assemble themselves to thee at the door of the tabernacle of the congregation.

Numbers 10:3

The first thing was that the blowing of the trumpet brought about the gathering of all of the camps. We have many camps and denominations, today, within the Body of Christ. We have camps with various beliefs and various traditions. But what God is doing in this Time Zone is giving out an invitation for all of God's camps to come together. The Church will not be successful, in this Time Zone being divided. The Church will be victorious and successful if we learn to stay united. The call is for all camps to unite under the prophetic anointing, canopy or mantle. I strongly believe that, in this endtime, the blowing of the prophetic trumpet will draw together all believers, irrespective of their denominations, religious backgrounds or agendas.

Men and women of God will be bound together with the cord of Love. Christians will be knitted together and remain under the canopy of the Lordship of Jesus. It will not be a compromising unity, but it will be one that is birthed from the prophetic anointing.

57

When ye blow an alarm, then the camps that lie on the east parts shall go forward.

When ye blow an alarm the second time, then the camps that lie on the south side shall take their journey: they shall blow an alarm for their journeys.

Numbers 10:5-6

The second purpose was that the trumpet was blown for the people to move. It was a sound of advancement. The Church has been complacent long enough. We have been too comfortable in our starchy, traditional ways. The prophetic trumpets are being blown in the land for God's people to move. We must move from our prayerless state to a life of spending quality time with the Lord. Because we have become comfortable with our old tools, our old ideas, our old strategies and our sinful attitude, we have become stagnant in the *things* of God. The Church of the 90s must move from its train of tradition and lukewarmness. We must start studying the Word and being doers of the Word. The things of God must become a great interest and concern to the Body of Christ today.

The Church must throw away the "old jaw bone" that used to be new, but now is old. There is a new one for this Time Zone. But in order to receive it, we will have to move with the sound produced by the prophetic trumpet.

This is what God is calling the Church toward in this Time Zone. The Church must move forward and not backward. The Body of Christ has been in bondage too long. It is high time for every individual to arise from his or her slumber and know that the trumpet has been blown, and the interpretation is "move forward, Church." God is calling every Christian to move into new realms within the Spirit. The Church is called in this Zone to tread where none has ever tread before, and that is the realm of the "super supernatural." We have seen and witnessed the "supernatural."

58

But, it is now time to move forward and make a science out of flowing in the "super supernatural." This would demand understanding the present Time Zone of God, obedience, dedication, holiness and commitment to God. There is a price to pay. We must be totally "sold out."

And if ye go to war in your land against the enemy that oppresseth you, then ye shall blow an alarm with the trumpets; and ye shall be remembered before the Lord your God, and ye shall be saved from your enemies.

Numbers 10:9

The third purpose was that the trumpet was blown to remind the people that it was time for war. We must remember that it is the time when kings go to war. It is not a new war. It is an old war, where the victory has already been accomplished for the Church. But we have a responsibility, and it is to maintain the victory that Christ wrought for us at Calvary. We must learn to demonstrate the defeat of the devil consistently in our lives. Not one time victorious and another time defeated. The Church must not allow the enemy to have ascendancy over Her. The prophetic trumpet is being blown in this Zone because there are a lot of Christians still at ease at Zion. We need to be awakened from our sleep. We need to wake up and smell the coffee. Ministers, leaders of churches and ministries, must arise and train their congregations about the urgency of this new move of the Spirit of God, and a need to move with it.

Just like as old, God is raising up an army for Himself. An army that will be well skilled in all of the instruments and tools of God. An army that will not be afraid of the tricks, devices and strategies of his enemy. I am talking about an army that has been well trained in the cave called "Adullam." The "Cave Adullam" is the place where purpose is found and redefined. It was the place of training for David's powerful and formidable armies.

I believe that the prophetic trumpet is being blown in the land by the prophets and apostles for men and women who possess such calibre and quality to enlist. The question is, have you been enlisted or are you still waiting to be enlisted? It may be too late. Now is the appointed time. This is an hour of warfare and confrontation with the kingdom of the enemy. The "certain" sound of the prophetic trumpet has been blown. But, we must rightfully interpret the sound.

Also in the day of your gladness, and in your solemn days, and in the beginnings of your months, ye shall blow with the trumpets over your burnt offerings, and over the sacrifices of your peace offerings; that they may be to you for a memorial before your God: I *am* the Lord your God.

Numbers 10:10

Then shalt thou cause the trumpet of the jubilee to sound on the tenth *day* of the seventh month, in the day of atonement shall ye make the trumpet sound throughout all your land.

Leviticus 25:9

Finally, the purpose for the blowing of the trumpet was for announcing spiritual demands and for the celebration of the feasts. Just like the Old Testament, the prophetic trumpet, today, is calling the Church to a style of life that is acceptable unto God. The trumpet is being blown for the final feast, which is the Feast of the Tabernacles. God is about to restore in full the Tabernacle of David, in its entirety. The house of Jacob will possess their possessions again. The four breaches of the Tabernacle will be restored back unto the Tabernacle.

The Valley of Bones versus
the Valley of Lives

The hand of the Lord was upon me, and carried me out in the spirit of the Lord, and set me down in the midst of the valley which *was* full of bones,

And caused me to pass by them round about: and, behold, *there were* very many in the open valley; and, lo, *they were* very dry.

And he said unto me, Son of man, can these bones live? And I answered, O Lord God, thou knowest.

Again he said unto me, Prophesy upon these bones, and say unto them, O ye dry bones, hear the word of the Lord.

Thus saith the Lord God unto these bones; Behold, I will cause breath to enter into you, and ye shall live:

And I will lay sinews upon you, and will bring up flesh upon you, and cover you with skin, and put breath in you, and ye shall live; and ye shall know that I *am* the Lord.

So I prophesied as I was commanded: and as I prophesied, there was a noise, and behold a shaking, and the bones came together, bone to his bone.

And when I beheld, lo, the sinews and the flesh came up upon them, and the skin covered them above: but *there was* no breath in them.

Then said he unto me, Prophesy unto the wind, prophesy, son of man, and say to the wind, Thus saith the Lord God; Come from the four winds. O breath, and breathe upon these slain, that they may live.

So I prophesied as he commanded me, and the breath came into them, and they lived, and stood up upon their feet, an exceeding great army.

Then he said unto me, Son of man, these bones are the whole house of Israel: behold, they say, Our bones are dried, and our hope is lost: we are cut off for our parts.

Ezekiel 37:1-11

These Scriptures draw the prophetic picture which actually describes the events discussed above. The prophet was caused to see a valley of dry bones; the bones were very many and very dry. These represented God's people. The prophet was twice asked whether he thought these bones could live again, and twice he referred the question back to the Lord. On each occasion, the prophet is to prophesy on these bones, which he did with the accompanying results.

The repeated injunction "prophesy, son of man ... so I prophesied" is similar to blowing the trumpet, because it could have been "Blow, son of man ... so I blew." The two blowings would belong to the two silver trumpets. Many have heard the first blowing of the prophetic trumpet. Believers are now coming back home. Men and women who have lived in the valley of dead bones are being restored back to their original state. Christians who have been spiritually dead have been awakened from their dry and dead state by the prophetic sound that the trumpet produces.

It is not finished yet, there is a prophetic trumpet that is still blowing within this Time Zone to put a prophetic breath into the lives of every Christian that has heard the prophetic sound. Not only will they receive a prophetic breath, but God wants to build up a fresh living army, men and women that are not afraid and intimidated by their foes.

The first prophetic sound across the land produced flesh, sinew and skin upon the lives of Christians that were spiritually dried up and dead. I strongly believe that, in this Time Zone of the Spirit of God, the prophetic sound that is being echoed is calling the Church to be enlisted into this endtime living army. An army that not only knows about warfare, but an army that knows about worship, prayer, fasting, holiness and has a great appetite and desire to please their commander (God) in every facet of their lives.

The New Wine versus the Old Wine

Awake, ye drunkards, and weep; and howl, all ye drinkers of wine, because of the new wine; for it is cut off from your mouth.

For a nation is come up upon my land, strong, and without number, whose teeth *are* the teeth of a lion, and he hath the cheek teeth of a great lion.

He hath laid my vine waste, and barked my fig tree: he hath made it clean bare, and cast *it* away; the branches thereof are made white.

Lament like a virgin girded with sackcloth for the husband of her youth.

The meat offering and the drink offering is cut off from the house of the Lord; the priest, the Lord's ministers, mourn.

The field is wasted, the land mourneth; for the corn is wasted: the new wine is dried up, the oil languisheth.

Be ye ashamed, O ye husbandmen; howl, O ye vine-dressers, for the wheat and for the barley; because the harvest of the field is perished.

The vine is dried up, and the fig tree languisheth; the pomegranate tree, the palm tree also, and the apple tree, *even* all the trees of the field, are withered: because joy is withered away from the sons of men.

Gird yourselves, and lament, ye priests: howl, ye ministers of the altar: come, lie all night in sackcloth, ye ministers of my God: for the meat offering and the drink offering is withholden from the house of your God.

Sanctify ye a fast, call a solemn assembly, gather the elders *and* all the inhabitants of the land *into* the house of the Lord your God, and cry unto the Lord.

Alas for the day! For the day of the Lord *is* at hand, and as a destruction from the Almighty shall it come.

Joel 1:5-15

When you look at this Scripture, you will see that it is divided into different parts. In the first part, I hear God calling the Church to AWAKE and weep, and to howl and to intercede, because the new wine is cut off from the mouth of the Church. The Body of Christ needs to awaken from its slumber. We have been sleeping long enough. It is time for the Body of Christ to take up their pallets and WALK.

The Church needs to weep and howl over our cities, our towns, our countries, our meetings and services because of the lack of new wine. All the Church has been experiencing is the old wine. We need the new wine. The new wine was cut off because men and women would not obey God and walk in His Commandments. Our churches have been dried up, and are sour and stinking. We have dry bones sitting in our pews and mounting our pulpits, because of the lack of this new wine. The old wine was good, but it was not the best. It is time for the new wine. Many Christians are dried up and lack this wine, and do not even know it. Many have gone long enough without this new oil. There is a cry for a change. It is time for an oil change. We need to go to the chief mechanic (God), and get our oil changed and ourselves tuned up for this new season.

The other thing we see in this Scripture is that God tells us how to go about receiving and bringing in this new wine. In order to do this, the Bible lets us know that we must "sanctify ye a fast." We must call a solemn assembly, gather all the elders, the deacons, the ushers and the board members, the ministry of helps members, the bishops, the mamas

64

and the papas of the Church, and all of the lay people together to a fast unto the Lord. This is what our churches must do. We must cry out for this new wine. We must let Him know that the old wine is finished and that we need new wine for the feast. We must not leave His presence until we have been filled up to the brim with this new wine. We must persist and hold on to the horn of God's altar until the new wine is rained upon us, our churches, our ministers, our traditions, our cities, our countries and our nations. We must demand that justice flow like a river, and righteousness like an overflowing stream.

Blow ye the trumpet in Zion, and sound an alarm in my holy mountain: let all the inhabitants of the land tremble: for the day of the Lord cometh, for *it is* **nigh at hand.**

Joel 2:1

There are many who still cannot hear what God is saying because they do not know that the trumpet is being blown. Still, many hear the sound of the prophetic trumpet, and are unable to respond to this solemn gathering because they are unable to interpret the meaning of the sound being echoed.

The prophetic trumpet is continually being blown by the prophets and the apostles whom God has raised to pioneer this move in this Time Zone. We must listen to them and interpret what God is saying through the sound that they are producing, "For the day of the Lord cometh, for it is nigh at hand." You cannot be a part of this solemn assembly and gathering if you are unable to interpret the prophetic sound that is being echoed in the land today.

The Church's obedience to this sound will bring God's people to a position and a place of receiving the new wine. The question is, are you satisfied with the old wine? Or do you need new wine, new oil and new refreshment from the presence of God? If your answer is yes, then join the train and respond to the prophetic sound that is being blown in the land by the prophets.

So I challenge you, child of God, can you, first of all, hear anything? And if so, what do you hear, just a "noise" or the "sound" of the prophetic trumpet? Do you have what it takes to react, to recognize and to interpret what is being heard?

Chapter IV

The Vow of the Nazarites

And the Lord spake unto Moses, saying,

Speak unto the children of Israel, and say unto them, When either man or woman shall separate *themselves* to vow a vow of a Nazarite, to separate *themselves* unto the Lord.

He shall separate *himself* from wine and strong drink, and shall drink no vinegar of wine, or vinegar of strong drink, neither shall he drink any liquor of grapes, nor eat moist grapes, or dried.

All the days of his separation shall he eat nothing that is made of the vine tree, from the kernels even to the husk.

All the days of the vow of his separation there shall no razor come upon his head: until the days be fulfilled, in the which he separateth *himself* unto the Lord, he shall be holy, *and* shall let the locks of the hair of his head grow.

All the days that he separateth *himself* unto the Lord he shall come at no dead body.

He shall not make himself unclean for his father, or for his mother, for his brother, or for his sister, when they die: because the consecration of his God *is* upon his head.

All the days of his separation he *is* holy unto the Lord.

And if any man die very suddenly by him, and he hath defiled the head of his consecration; then he shall shave his head in the day of his cleansing, on the seventh day shall he shave it.

And on the eighth day he shall bring two turtles, or two young pigeons, to the priest, to the door of the tabernacle of the congregation:

And the priest shall offer the one for a sin offering, and the other for a burnt offering, and make an atonement for him, for that he sinned by the dead, and shall hollow his head that same day.

And he shall consecrate unto the Lord the days of his separation, and shall bring a lamb of the first year for a trespass offering: but the days that were before shall be lost, because his separation was defiled.

And this *is* the law of the Nazarite, when the days of his separation are fulfilled: he shall be brought unto the door of the tabernacle of the congregation:

And he shall offer his offering unto the Lord, one he lamb of the first year without blemish for a burnt offering, and one ewe lamb of the first year without blemish for a sin offering, and one ram without blemish for peace offerings,

And a basket of unleavened bread, cakes of fine flour mingled with oil, and wafers of unleavened bread anointed with oil, and their meat offering, and their drink offerings.

And the priest shall bring *them* before the Lord, and shall offer his sin offering, and his burnt offering.

Numbers 6:1-16

I believe that the Body of Christ in this Time Zone is being called out to take the "vow of the Nazarite." This endtime Church will be a type of the Old Testament Nazarite. They will be a group of people with a longing to please God, and a group of people that will be ready and prepared to take up the cross and follow the Master. They will abide by Kingdom principles and Kingdom rules. They will walk in the law of the spirit of life in Christ Jesus, and not the law of sin and death. They will be men and women who know how to pummel their bodies and put their flesh

68

under subjection. They may not abide to the Old Testament commands of the Nazarite, but they will abide by the New Testament commands of what is expected of them by their Master.

The word, Nazarite, or spelled Nazirite, comes from the Hebrew word, "Nazar," meaning "consecrated," and the word "consecrated" means "to set apart as sacred"; it means to be dedicated to sacred uses. It also means to separate one's life to a cause. It means to present yourself holy and acceptable. This peculiar vow is one of total separation. God never forces anyone to do it. The vow is taken voluntarily, just as our new birth is voluntarily received.

A Nazarite was an Israelite who consecrated himself or herself, and took a vow of separation and self-imposed abstinence for the sole purpose of service unto the living God. It was taken by those who wanted to progress to higher degrees of God. The vows were for various lengths of time, anywhere from 30 to 60 days. Only a few are on record as lasting a lifetime — such as the experience of Samson (Judges 13:5-7, 16:17); Samuel (I Samuel 11:11); and John the Baptist (Luke 1:5). Samson is called a Nazarite, but Samuel and John were not so named. Only the law of the Nazarite applied to them. Paul once took a Nazarite vow.

This is what God is calling for in the Church today. God is calling for total separation from the things of the world. God is calling the Church to shun the works of the flesh and every appearance of evil. He is calling the Church to a complete consecration and separation.

The Commands of the Nazarite

■ A Nazarite must separate himself from wine and strong drink.

■ A Nazarite must not drink vinegar of wine

- Or vinegar of strong drink

- Or liquor of grapes.

- He shall not eat ripe grapes

- Or dried grapes.

- He shall eat nothing made of the vine, from the kernel to the husk.

- A Nazarite shall have no razor come upon his head during his Nazariteship.

- He shall be holy.

- He shall not be defiled for the dead, even for father, mother, sister or brother.

> **I beseech you therefore, brethren, by the mercies of God, that ye present your bodies a living sacrifice, holy, acceptable unto God, *which is* your reasonable service.**
>
> **And be not conformed to this world: but be ye transformed by the renewing of your mind, that ye may prove what *is* that good, and acceptable, and perfect, will of God.**

Romans 12:1-2

Like the Old Testament Nazarites, God is calling the Church to "present our bodies a living sacrifice, holy, acceptable unto God ..." Our bodies must be recognized as temples of the Holy Spirit and made holy by the indwelling Spirit. We should present them to our Father, not as a deed, but as a living sacrifice. This is a service that comes with great profit.

Just as the Old Testament Nazarite made vows, the Body of Christ must make new commitments to serve God faithfully. God is demanding that the Church be not conformed to this age, its fashions, customs, maxims and sinful practices. We must be changed and transfigured in spirit, soul and body by the recasting of our minds, which can only be done through the power of the Holy Spirit.

Love not the world, neither the things *that are* in the world. If any man love the world, the love of the Father is not in him.

For all that *is* in the world, the lust of the flesh, and the lust of the eyes, and the pride of life, is not of the Father, but is of the world.

And the world passeth away, and the lust thereof: but he that doeth the will of God abideth for ever.

I John 2:15-17

We must decide who we want to serve, Baal or Yaweh. It is time to stop hanging and dangling between two opinions, not sure of what to do. We must make up our minds once and for all to serve the Lord. We must take fresh, new vows to separate ourselves from the world's overload. We must avoid the lust of the flesh, the lust of the eyes and the pride of life.

I strongly believe that God is looking for a remnant in this hour who, like the Old Testament Nazarite, will make up their minds and "vow" to go all the way for the Lord, not for 30 to 60 days, but until Jesus returns. Men and women who will be sold out to God.

The Command for the New Testament Nazarite

If ye then be risen with Christ, seek those things which are above, where Christ sitteth on the right hand of God.

Set your affection on things above, not on things on the earth.

For ye are dead, and your life is hid with Christ in God.

When Christ, *who is* our life, shall appear, then shall ye also appear with him in glory.

Mortify therefore your members which are upon the earth; fornication, uncleanness, inordinate affection, evil concupiscence, and covetousness, which is idolatry:

For which things' sake the wrath of God cometh on the children of disobedience:

In the which ye also walked some time, when ye lived in them.

But now ye also put off all these; anger, wrath, malice, blasphemy, filthy communication out of your mouth.

Lie not one to another, seeing that ye have put off the old man with his deeds;

And have put on the new *man*, which is renewed in knowledge after the image of him that created him:

Put on therefore, as the elect of God, holy and beloved, bowels of mercies, kindness, humbleness of mind, meekness, long-suffering;

Forbearing one another, and forgiving one another, if any man have a quarrel against any: even as Christ forgave you, so also *do* ye.

And above all these things *put on* charity, which is the bond of perfectness.

And let the peace of God rule in your hearts, to the which also ye are called in one body; and be ye thankful.

Let t...

...you richly in all wisdom; teaching and ...s and hymns and spiritual songs, singing ...ord.

...r deed, *do* all in the name of the Lord ...he father by him.

Colossians 3:1-10,12-17

...wherewith Christ hath made us free, and ...oke of bondage.

...it, and ye shall not fulfill the lust of the

...pirit, and the Spirit against the flesh: and ...ther: so that ye cannot do the things that

...re not under the law.

...e manifest, which are *these*; Adultery, ...sness,

...nce, emulations, wrath, strife, seditions,

...revellings, and such like: of the which I ...*you* in time past, that they which do such ...m of God.

Bu ...e, joy, peace, long suffering, gentleness, goo

Meekness, temperance: against such there is no law.

And they that are Christ's have crucified the flesh with the affections and lusts.

Rosa Parks

born 1913
Civil Rights Activist

When Rosa Parks refused to give up her seat on a racially segregated bus in Montgomery, Alabama on December 1, 1955, she became a symbol of courageous resistance in the civil rights movement. "Tired of giving in," Parks' act of bravery led to a boycott and to important changes in the law within the decade. In 1999, she was awarded the Congressional Gold Medal, the nation's highest civilian honor.

If we live in the Spirit, let us also walk in the Spirit.

Let us not be desirous of vain glory, provoking one another, envying one another.

Galatians 5:1,16-26

And beside this, giving all diligence, add to your faith virtue; and to virtue knowledge;

And to knowledge temperance; and to temperance patience; and to patience godliness;

And to godliness brotherly kindness; and to brotherly kindness charity.

For if these things be in you, and abound, they make *you that ye shall* neither *be* barren nor unfruitful in the knowledge of our Lord Jesus Christ.

But he that lacketh these things is blind, and cannot see afar off, and hath forgotten that he was purged from his old sins.

II Peter 1:5-9

Just as the Old Testament Nazarite had a vow and commandments to keep, the New Testament Nazarite has its commandments to abide by. There are two key phrases that we will consider in these Scriptures — "the works of the flesh" and "the fruit of the Spirit." We will take each and carefully examine what the works of the flesh are and what the fruits of the Spirit are. The Scripture in II Peter 1 tells us that "if these things be in you, and abound, they make you that ye shall neither be barren nor unfruitful in the knowledge of our Lord Jesus Christ. But he that lacketh these things is blind, and cannot see ...."

We have been risen with Christ by the virtue of our new birth. So we must seek those things which are above and of God. This New Testament Nazarite is being commanded to put to death fornication, uncleanness,

74

inordinate affection, evil concupiscence and idolatry. We are being commanded to put to death the works of the flesh. We must put off malice, anger, wrath, blasphemy and filthy communication. We must then "put on," as separated and consecrated people, bowels of mercies, kindness, humbleness of mind, meekness, long-suffering; forbearing one another, and forgiving one another (if any man have a quarrel against any), we must walk in the fruit of the Spirit.

Works of the Flesh

- **Adultery and Fornication:** This involves an unlawful sexual relation between men and women, single and married.

- **Uncleanness:** Uncleanness is the opposite of purity; this includes sodomy, homosexuality, lesbianism, pederasty, bestiality and all other forms of sexual perversion.

- **Lasciviousness:** It is the promoting and partaking of that which tends to produce lewd emotions; anything tending to foster sex, sin and lust.

- **Idolatry:** Idolatry includes anything on which affections are passionately set, and an extravagant admiration of the heart. (Ephesians 5:5, Col 3:5).

- **Witchcraft:** Sorcery. The practice of dealing with evil spirits, magical incantations, and casting spells and charms upon one by means of drugs and potions of various kinds.

- **Hatred:** Bitter dislike, abhorrence, malice, and ill will against anyone. Tendency to hold grudges against, or be angry at, someone.

- **Variance:** Dissensions, discord, quarrelling, debating and disputes.

- **Emulation:** Envies, jealousies; striving to excel at the expense of another, seeking to surpass and outdo others; uncurbed rivalry spirit in religion, business, society and other fields of endeavor.

- **Wrath:** Turbulent passions, domestic and civil turmoils, rage, determined and lasting anger.

- **Strife:** Contention, disputation, contest for superiority or advantage, strenuous endeavors to equal or revenge the wrongs done to one.

- **Seditions:** Divisions, parties and factions; popular disorder, stirring up strife in religion, government, home or any other place.

- **Envying:** Pain, ill will and jealousy at the good fortune or blessing of another.

- **Murders:** To kill, to spoil or mar the happiness of another.

- **Drunkenness:** Living intoxicated, a slave to drink, drinking bouts.

- **Revelling:** Rioting, lascivious and boisterous feastings, with obscene music and other sinful activities, pleasures, and carousings.

Fruit of the Spirit

The Fruit of the Spirit are as follows:

- **Love:** This is the agape kind of the love. It is a divine love. It is a strong, ardent, tender, compassionate, devotion to the well-being of someone.

- **Joy:** The emotional excitement, gladness, delight over blessings received or expected for oneself and for others.

- **Peace:** The state of quietness, rest, repose, harmony, order and security in the midst of turmoil, strife and temptations.

- **Long-suffering:** Patient endurance, to bear long with the frailties, offenses, injuries and provocations of others, without murmuring, repining or resentment.

- **Gentleness:** A disposition to be gentle, soft-spoken, kind, even-tempered, cultured and refined in character and conduct.

- **Goodness:** The state of being good, kind, virtuous, benevolent, generous and God-like in life and conduct.

- **Faith:** The Greek word for faith is "pistis." It is the living, divinely implanted, acquired and created principle of inward and wholehearted confidence, assurance, trust and reliance in God and all that He says.

- **Meekness:** The disposition to be gentle, kind, indulgent, even-balanced in tempers and passions, and patient in suffering injuries without feeling or spirit of revenge.

- **Temperance:** Self-control, a moderation in the indulgence of the appetites and passions.

The Nazarite

Among the Jews, an abundance of hair was considered a mark of physical strength and perfection, and baldness a mark of physical imperfection. The free growth of hair on heads of Nazarites represented the dedication of a person with his whole strength and powers to the service of God. As was Delilah with Samson, the devil is using the lust of the flesh, the lust of the eyes and the pride of life to cut our hair. The spiritual Delilah's are being sown into the Church to cause us to compromise and lose our anointing. No anointing — no victory!

If a Nazarite touched a dead body, even accidentally, he was defiled and needed to shave his head and offer a sacrifice. The same applies to the Church today. When we sin or catch ourself in an act that is not of God, we must immediately repent of our sins. Sometimes believers go on sinning and never repent. It is like their conscience is dead. We must be quick to repent our sins, so that we can always receive new refreshings from God.

Let's look at one of the most popular Nazarites in the Bible.

And the children of Israel did evil again in the sight of the Lord; and the Lord delivered them into the hand of the Philistines forty years.

And there was a certain man of Zorah, of the family of the Danites, whose name *was* Manoah; and his wife *was* barren, and bare not.

And the angel of the Lord appeared unto the woman, and said unto her, Behold now, thou *art* barren, and bearest not: but thou shalt conceive, and bear a son.

Now therefore beware, I pray thee, and drink not wine nor strong drink, and eat not any unclean *thing*:

For, lo, thou shalt conceive, and bear a son; and no razor shall come on his head: for the child shall be a Nazarite unto God from the womb: And he shall begin to deliver Israel out of the hand of the Philistines.

Then the woman came and told her husband, saying, A man of God came unto me, and his countenance *was* like the countenance of an angel of God,

very terrible: but I asked him not whence he *was*, neither told he me his name:

But he said unto me, Behold thou shalt conceive, and bear a son; and now drink no wine nor strong drink, neither eat any unclean *thing*: for the child shall be a Nazarite to God from the womb to the day of his death.

Then Manoah entreated the Lord, and said, O my Lord, let the man of God which thou didst send come again unto us, and teach us what we shall do unto the child that shall be born.

Judges 13:1-8

And it came to pass afterward, that he loved a woman in the valley of Sorek, whose name *was* Delilah.

And the lords of the Philistines came up unto her, and said unto her, Entice him, and see wherein his great strength *lieth*, and by what *means* we may prevail against him, that we may bind him to afflict him: and we will give thee every one of us eleven hundred *pieces* of silver.

And Delilah said to Samson, Tell me, I pray thee, wherein thy great strength *lieth* and wherewith thou mightest be bound to afflict thee.

And Samson said unto her, If they bind me with seven green withs that were never dried, then shall I be weak, and be as another man.

Then the lords of the Philistines brought up to her seven green withs which had not been dried, and she bound him with them.

Now *there were* men lying in wait, abiding with her in the chamber. And she said unto him, The Philistines *be* upon thee, Samson. And he brake the withs, as a thread of tow is broken when it toucheth the fire. So his strength was not known.

And Delilah said unto Samson, Behold, thou hast mocked me, and told me lies: now tell me, I pray thee, wherewith thou mightest be bound.

And he said unto her, If they bind me fast with new ropes that never were occupied, then shall I be weak, and be as another man.

Delilah therefore took new ropes, and bound him therewith, and said unto him, the Philistines *be* upon thee, Samson. And *there were* liars in wait abiding in the chamber. And he brake them from off his arms like a thread.

And Delilah said unto Samson, Hitherto thou has mocked me, and told me lies: tell me wherewith thou mightest be bound. And he said unto her, If thou weavest the seven locks of my head with the web.

And it came to pass, when she pressed him daily with her words, and urged him, *so* that his soul has vexed unto death;

That the told her all his heart, and said unto her, There hath not come a razor upon mine head; for I *have been* a Nazarite unto God from my mother's womb: if I be shaven, then my strength will go from me, and I shall become weak, and be like any *other* man.

And when Delilah saw that he had told her all his heart, she sent and called for the lords of the Philistines, saying, Come up this once, for he hath shown me all his heart. Then the lords of the Philistines came up unto her, and brought money in their hand.

And she made him sleep upon her knees; and she called for a man and caused him to shave off the seven locks of his head; and she began to afflict him, and his strength went from him.

And she said, the Philistines *be* upon thee Samson. And he awoke out of his sleep, and said, I will go out as at other times before, and shake myself. And he wist not that the Lord was departed from him.

But the Philistines took him, and put out his eyes, and brought him down to Gaza, and bound him with fetters of brass; and he did grind in the prison house.

Howbeit the hair of his head began to grow again after he was shaven.

Then the lords of the Philistines gathered them together for to offer a great sacrifice unto Dagon their god, and to rejoice: for they said, Our god hath delivered Samson our enemy into our hand.

And when the people saw him, they praised their god: for they said, Our god hath delivered into our hands our enemy, and the destroyer of our country, which slew many of us.

And it came to pass, when their hearts were merry, that they said, Call for Samson, that he may make us sport. And they called for Samson out of the prison house; and he made them sport: and they set him between the pillars.

And Samson said unto the lad that held him by the hand, Suffer me that I may feel the pillars whereupon the house standeth, that I may lean upon them.

And Samson said, Let me die with the Philistines. And he bowed himself with *all his* might; and the house fell upon the lords, and upon all the people that *were* therein. So the dead which he slew at his death were more than *they* which he slew in his life.

Judges 16:4-13,16-26,30

The first Scriptures here tell us about the calling of Samson right from his mother's womb as a Nazarite. Samson was born with the vow of the Nazarite upon his life. As Samson grew, he experienced the Power of God constantly upon his life. But the demonstration of the Power of God upon his life was contingent upon his faithfulness and dedication to the vow of the Nazarite. As long as he was obedient to his vow, God kept His part of the deal. Samson defeated the Philistines and the enemies of Israel every time he went to war.

The Breaking of the Vow

But in the second Scripture, the Bible begins to tell us how Samson lost the anointing upon his life, because he had broken his vow. We begin

81

to see a different Samson here. The lust of the flesh and the lust of the eyes cost Samson his life. Samson's marriage to Delilah was the beginning of his downfall. God had already warned the Israelites not to marry the women of other nations. But Samson failed to adhere to this warning. He not only married a woman of another nation, he married an harlot. When we disobey God, there are certain consequences that we must pay. Samson's disobedience caused him to break the vow of the Nazarite.

The Samson Cycle

And the woman bare a son, and called his name Samson: and the child grew, and the Lord blessed him.

And the spirit of the Lord began to move him at times in the camp of Dan between Zorah and Eshtaol.

Judges 13:24-25

Notice that from a child the Spirit of God began to move on Samson. Samson did not workout at the local gym. His strength was not derived from a physical fitness program. What made Samson strong was something beyond the physical. Since a young boy, he kept the Nazarite vow and the vow of consecration, separation and holiness before God caused him to be under the anointing of the Holy Ghost. The Bible says that the Spirit of the Lord moved him. In Hebrew, that actual translation is "the Spirit of the Lord took possession of him." Many times, we think that the Holy Spirit has moved when a few people dance, fall out, shout and prophesy. That is part of it, but the moving of the Holy Spirit is when the Body of Christ comes into the unity of the Spirit in the bond of peace.

Token of His Vow

Samson's strength did not lie in his hair or in his muscles, as many may think, but in the relationship and contact he had with God. His hair was a token of his vow to God and spoke of that relationship which gave him strength. When he broke his vow, Samson awakened to a new world which he had never known — the world of defeat and failure. He realized that he was nothing without God. The same thing happens today. Many times, Christians sin and never take it serious. Many believers operate whatever lifestyle they like, failing to realize that without God we can do nothing.

Ichabod

Samson betrayed himself and his God, and dearly paid for his foolishness and sin. He could have easily seen that Delilah was determined to ruin him, but the weakness of his heart was stronger than the strength of his body. When he betrayed God, he experienced his first hair cut and the first razor to come upon his head.

He was no longer a Nazarite. He was as weak as other men, for his strength had left him. His enemies had power over him. The anointing, the glory and the favor of God immediately departed from him. This is exactly what happens when we betray God by the way we live our lives. The reasons most Christians are being defeated by the enemy is because they have failed to obey God. They have deviated from the purpose, the assignment and mandate upon their lives. When you deviate, you will pay dearly for it.

The God of Restoration and of a Second Chance

If we confess our sins, he is faithful and just to forgive us *our* **sins; and to cleanse us from all unrighteousness.**

I John 1:9

Thank God, God is a God of a second chance. He will be a God of many chances to you, if you want Him to be. Samson realized his mistake and foolishness. He realized that he had sinned against the most high God by breaking his vow. He asked God for another chance. His hair, which was a symbol of his covenant, began to grow back. Samson said **"O Lord God, remember me, I pray thee, only this once ...."** Samson repented of his sins and mistakes. He wanted another chance. He wanted a time of refreshing from the presence of the Lord. With refreshings comes deliverance, healings and victories.

God answered Samson. The Scripture lets us know that Samson experienced more exploits and won more victories in one day than he ever did in all the days of his life. That is the difference that the anointing brings. When we repent of our sins, God is happy to restore us back to a higher level and dimension in the Spirit.

The Power Is Coming Home

But the Philistines took him, and put out his eyes, and brought him down to Gaza, and bound him with fetters of brass; and he did grind in the prison house.

Judges 16:21

I believe, in this Time Zone, the Church will experience the coming home of the power of God. I don't care what the Church has gone through. I don't care what had happened to the Body of Christ. Our hair will grow again. The Church's hair is growing again.

Just as Samson's hair was growing again, the vow, the consecration, the holiness and the anointing are coming back to the Church. Even though Samson's eyes were plucked out, his hair began to grow again. No more women wanted him. He was now the rejected. He moved from being greatly known to being unknown. But as Samson's hair began to grow, his heart began to get strong. He began to realize that everything he had was not because he was Samson, but because he was anointed of God. I can hear Samson crying out, "Oh God, anoint me one more time," Hallelujah! His eyes were plucked out and the Philistines had made mockery of him.

The world has mocked the Church too long. The news media has disgraced the Church for too long. But I want you to know that the Church's hair is growing back again. When God is finished with this endtime Church, we will not look the same. We might have our eyes plucked out, we may not have the fancy clothes, we may be bloodied from the war, but our hair is growing again. The power is coming home.

> **By faith the harlot Rahab perished not with them that believed not, when she had received the spies with peace.**
>
> **And what shall I more say, for the time would fail me to tell of Gideon, and** *of* **Barak, and** *of* **Samson, and** *of* **Jephthae; of David also, and Samuel, and** *of* **the prophets:**
>
> **Who through faith subdued kingdoms, wrought righteousness, obtained promises, stopped the mouths of lions.**
>
> **Hebrews 11:31-33**

The greatest part of this story is found in this Scripture. Every denomination would have rejected Samson and excommunicated him. He would have never preached in their pulpits again. But God always moves in a different way. God is interested in repairing lives. God is repairing lives today, including preachers of the Gospel that have once missed it. Don't point your finger at anyone. God is in the restoring business. He is in the healing business, not just healing blind eyes and deaf ears, but healing broken spirits. Samson was lifted up out of the Philistine country, and God placed him on the honor roll of faith — from chaos and confusion to a crown of glory. This is the stage that the Church is going through today. The Church has gone through the chaos and the confusion stage, and now is the time for God to raise the Church to His honor roll. For this to happen, the Body of Christ must renew their vow — the vow of separation, consecration and holiness, and walk in it.

In this Time Zone of the Spirit of God, God is raising up men and women who have caught hold of His power. He is raising up men and women who have taken the vow of the Nazarite — the vow of separation, consecration and holiness. We can preach fancy sermons, but nothing will set people freer than the anointing of the Holy Ghost. God is calling for a holy (whole and complete) Church.

Many Christians desire to bind the devil when they, themselves, are still bound. Believers want to be equipped with the latest techniques of spiritual warfare when they, themselves, have not conquered the lust (pressure) of the flesh. We have several seminars on the gifts of the Spirit, but we forget that His name is holy. The Church needs to emphasize more the importance of sharing God's burden (responsibility) out of a broken heart, rather than five carnal principles.

Thou blind Pharisee, cleanse first that *which is* within the cup and platter, that the outside of them may be clean also.

Matthew 23:26

It is not what we appear to one another that counts. It is not what we put on the outside that matters. It is what is in our heart that God is looking at. This is the reason that there has been a lack of revival in the land. But, in this Time Zone, God is raising up men and women who will place great emphasis on walking right before Him. They will take the vow of the Nazarite to separate themselves from the ways of the world. Their primary concern will be to please God in every area of their lives.

There is no shortcut to this. There is no seminar or workshop that we can attend which will make us into what God is calling for in this hour. What God needs is men and women who will lay down on their faces before Him. The Church has gone through many cycles. The Church went through the power cycle in the "Charismatic Renewal." Then we moved into the "Word Cycle," where people are saying, "Praise God, we don't dance like that anymore, we just study the Word." The Church went from all power to no power. All we do now is learn techniques, phrases and catchy cliches. These will not bring God onto the scene. We need God on the scene every moment. We need the power of God and we need the Word. Once we get the power and the Word, the Body of Christ will grow.

Subduing the Flesh

What God is interested in, in this Time Zone, is the vow — the consecration, holiness and the separation. The story of Samson is one of a man who started out in God, went through chaos and returned back to God.

No, I beat my body and make it my slave so that after I have preached to others, I myself will not be disqualified for the prize.

I Corinthians 9:27 (NIV)

The Body of Christ has a lot of "reject" ministers of the Gospel who have not beaten themselves down and taken themselves from the crowd and apart from the limelight. Samson started out with the anointing of the Holy Spirit in his life. When we reach chapter fourteen of Judges, we find him looking to the Philistines for a wife. You see, child of God, you cannot do God's business and be married to the world.

Samson had been where he should not have been, seeing what he should not have seen, doing what he should not have done and, yet, God in His mercy and grace moved upon him. The Spirit of the Lord would come mightily upon Samson, and he would grab a lion and, as like renting a little kid or a little goat, he would rip it apart. That was not Samson's strength. It was the anointing of the Holy Ghost. One sin led to another. Samson went down and down. On the outside, Samson looked the same. We can look the same on the outside, putting on the "make-up" of religion. We can make it look and sound good.

Samson finally was laying with his head on the lap of Delilah. After several attempts by Delilah to learn the secret of Samson's strength, Samson finally gave in. He said, "it's my hair, if you cut my hair, I am like any other man." You see, child of God, practicing sin day by day behind closed doors, when nobody sees it, becomes habitual. There will no longer be consecration in the heart. The "honey will be taken out of the carcass."

When Samson realized what had happened, he thought he could just go out and shake himself as before. But the anointing was gone. The devil will make fun of you when you have yielded to sin.

Living a Life of Holiness

In those days *there was* **no king in Israel,** *but* **every man did** *that which was* **right in his own eyes.**

Judges 17:6

Because of man walking in disobedience, we find seven stages in the book of Judges. The people of God fell into sin, they became servitude, then they repented, then they were restored back on target again. Seven times these stages repeated themselves in the Book of Judges. But God, in His mercy, will always raise somebody up to deliver His people and, most of the time, the sent deliverer is always the *unknown.*

God will raise up an *Unknown* to get the known done. God, in this hour, is raising up many Unknowns, so that the known can be fully executed. Jephthat and Gideon were examples of the unknown in the Bible.

And the angel of the Lord appeared unto him, and said unto him, The Lord *is* **with thee, thou mighty man of valour.**

Judges 6:12

The angel of God looked down, the unknown was on the threshing floor, hiding, threshing wheat. The angel of the Lord said to Gideon, "Gideon thou mighty man of valor." Gideon's reply was, "Are you talking to me? I am the poorest of the poor. My family is the lowest of the low." Gideon was one of the unknowns. But God was interested in him. I believe that, in this hour, many unknowns will be raised up by God in their various neighborhoods, cities, countries and nations. They will be raised up to declare the known. But one outright characteristic that will be a quality of these people will be that they have taken the vow of the Nazarite.

Going the Way of the Flesh or Having God's Power Flowing through You

The purpose of God's anointing in this hour is to CHANGE the Body of Christ. When Samuel anointed Saul, he told him, "This anointing is going to change you." When the anointing came, it came with the purpose of changing. The Body of Christ has a big decision to make. Do you want to go the way of the flesh, or do you want to latch hold of something in the spirit world.

> Now Naaman, captain of the host of the King of Syria, was a great man with his master, and honourable, because by him the Lord had given deliverance unto Syria: he was also a mighty man in valour, *but he was* a leper.
>
> And the Syrians had gone out by companies, and had brought away captive out of the land of Israel a little maid; and she waited on Naaman's wife.
>
> And she said unto her mistress, Would God my lord *were* with the prophet that *is* in Samaria! for he would recover him of his leprosy.
>
> **II Kings 5:1-3**

Imagine the incredible words that came out of the mouth of the maid. If she gave this testimony in most of our churches today, she might be thrown out. The first thing we would do is to criticize her and say, "What are you doing, sending somebody to a man?" The next thing we would say is that, "Don't you know that no man has the power to heal?" We have many Pentecostal preachers hiding behind the press today.

90

Swimming in the Jordan River versus Swimming in the Abana and Pharpar Rivers

The Body of Christ who have taken this vow has a choice to make, whether to stay in the rut of the harvest or to cut our shorelines.

And *one* went in, and told his lord, saying, Thus and thus said the maid that *is* of the land of Israel.

And the king of Syria said, Go to, go, and I will send a letter unto the king of Israel. And he departed, and took with him ten talents of silver, and six thousand *pieces* of gold, and ten changes of raiment.

And he brought the letter to the king of Israel, saying, Now when this letter is come unto thee, behold, I have *therewith* sent Naaman my servant to thee, that thou mayest recover him of his leprosy.

And it came to pass, when the king of Israel had read the letter, that he rent his clothes, and said, *Am* I God, to kill and to make alive, that this man doth send unto me to recover a man of his leprosy? wherefore consider, I pray you, and see how he seeketh a quarrel against me.

And it was *so*, when Elisha the man of God had heard that the king of Israel had rent his clothes, that he sent to the king, saying, Wherefore hast thou rent thy clothes? let him come now to me, and he shall know that there is a prophet in Israel.

Now Naaman came with his horses and with his chariot, and stood at the door of the house of Elisha.

And Elisha sent a messenger unto him, saying, Go and wash in Jordan seven times, and thy flesh shall come again to thee, and thou shalt be clean.

But Naaman was wroth, and went away, and said, Behold, I thought, He will surely come out to me, and stand, and call on the name of the Lord his God, and strike his hand over the place, and recover the leper.

II Kings 5:4-11

Naaman was angry at Elisha. He went away and said, "I thought he surely is going to come out and wave his magical hand over me and call on the name of the Lord, strike his hand over this place and recover my leprosy."

Listen to what Naaman said, "There are two rivers here in Damascus. I don't understand it. He wants me to go wash in the Jordan. Doesn't he know that is a stinky, dirty, smelly place?"

Are **not Abana and Pharpar, rivers of Damascus, better than all the waters of Israel? may I not wash in them, and be clean? So he turned and went away in a rage.**

II Kings 5:12

The problem, today, is that the Church wants to swim in the river where there is no power. The literal meaning of "*Abana*" is "Human Might." Pharpar means "Human Sufficiency." Naaman wanted to swim in the water of man's ability, human sufficiency, but there is no anointing there. Many Christians are swimming today in the Abana and Pharpar Rivers. It is not surprising that many Christians are suffering from spiritual leprosy. Swimming in the river of human might and man-made help will cause the Body of Christ to develop spiritual leprosy.

There is something about these rivers. The Abana and Pharpar Rivers are very clean in comparison to the Jordan River. Their waters are so clean that it is enticing. Many Christians and leaders within the Body of Christ have been enticed to swim in it. The reason a lot of Christians and leaders are experiencing spiritual leprosy today is because they have been swimming for too long in these rivers.

The Church needs a change. But, in order to receive a change, we must be willing to swim in the Jordan River, which is muddy and unclean. Jordan means "death." It is the river of God. As we begin to swim in the Jordan River, what we are doing is making quality decisions to "put to death" every work of the flesh that has caused spiritual leprosy in our lives. As we begin to swim in the Jordan River, we are simply saying that we are tired of going by our own strength and effort, and we are turning it over to God. We must put aside our pride, our egos, and positions, and humble ourselves under the mighty hand of God. When Naaman made up his mind to swim in the Jordan River seven times, he was changed. He was cured of his leprosy. His skin became like the skin of a young baby. That is what happens when we swim in the Jordan River. Our lives, our ways and our attitudes are changed for God. Let's swim, Church, in the Jordan River, instead of swimming in the Abana and Pharpar Rivers. I believe strongly that, in this Time Zone, the men and women who have taken the vow of the Nazarite will yearn to swim as never before in the Jordan River of our generation.

Individuals who have taken the vow will run far from the Abana and Pharpar Rivers to dip in the Jordan River. If we are going to flow in this move of the Spirit of God, we must get into the river of God. That is the only place where the supernatural flows. The arm of flesh will not provide the answer to the movement of God during this Time Zone. The answer will come from a life that is touched, transformed, made new and recreated with the power of the Holy Spirit.

Chapter V

Developing the Spirit of Excellence

There is a call in this hour for men and women of character and excellence. The Body of Christ, for sometime, has been plagued with individuals whose character have been assassinated. God is requiring excellence in this hour. Everything that we do must be excellent. We must walk in excellence in our personal lives. We must walk in excellence in our ministries and in power with God. You get good results when you walk in the spirit of excellence. Excellence and character work hand-in-hand. We cannot develop the spirit of excellence without first working on our character. So when we talk of excellence, we are also talking about character and vice versa. The spirit of excellence actually permeates from good character.

The Church must walk in the rhythm of excellence. God does not need slouched, timid and fearful people in these last days. God needs people that are bold in Him. Child of God, listen, if you walk in integrity, reverence and in honesty, you will never have to worry about walking in the spirit of excellence. Why? Because the word, "integrity," in the Hebrew and Greek means "prosperity." When you walk in integrity, you are walking in prosperity. When you walk in integrity, God will always send someone across your path to bless you. You literally walk in living prosperity. When you walk in integrity, God will always cause you to walk in excellence. The word, "excellent" in Hebrew means "preeminent" or "outstanding."

The reason most needs are not met today in our churches is because there is a great lack of integrity and reverence. The breastplate of integrity covers our heart. Once there is no integrity, you are exposed to the deceptions of the devil. The spirit of reverence is what draws the presence of God down to wherever you want Him to be. When there is no integrity, you allow the enemy to run around the scene, and when there is no reverence, God is not on the scene, and when God is not on the scene, you are bound to fail.

God's purpose for the Church is to bring many sons to glory. For the Church to reach this goal, Her leaders must lead the way. The leaders of the Church must be the first partakers of the glorious plan of God in maturing His sons. He must develop the character and personality of the Lord Jesus in the Church leaders before he can form it in His people at large. Many churches have emphasized the gifts and power of a leader, far above his character development. This imbalance has caused many problems within the Church, including the backsliding of many leaders. Today, however, God is bringing us back to a balance between gifts and character. The Lord is not concerned with a leader's gift and anointing only. He also cares deeply about our lifestyle and character. Many so-called gifted and anointed men of God have fallen flat on their faces because they have no character and refused to walk in the spirit of excellence. God desires a great balance between gifts and character in every one of our lives.

Andre Maurois said these words, **"If you create an act, you create a habit. If you create a habit, you create a character ... If you create a character, you create a destiny."** D.L. Moody said this, **"If I take care of my character, my reputation will take care of itself"** and Aristotle said, **"To enjoy the things we ought, and to hate the things we ought, has the greatest bearing on excellence of character."** You see, character is like a tree, and reputation and excellence is like its shadow. The shadow is what we think of it, but only the tree has the substance of reality.

And when the queen of Sheba heard of the fame of Solomon, she came to prove Solomon with hard questions at Jerusalem, with a very great company, and camels that bare spices, and gold in abundance, and precious stones: and when she was come to Solomon, she communed with him of all that was in her heart.

And Solomon told her all her questions: and there was nothing hid from Solomon which he told her not,

And when the queen of Sheba had seen the wisdom of Solomon, and the house that he had built,

And the meat of his table, and the sitting of his servants, and the attendance of his ministers, and their apparel; his cupbearers also, and their apparel; and his ascent by which he went up into the house of the Lord; there was no more spirit in her.

And she said to the king, *It was* a true report which I heard in mine own land of thine acts, and of thy wisdom;

Howbeit I believed not their words, until I came, and mine eyes had seen *it*: and, behold, the one half of the greatness of thy wisdom was not told me: *for* thou exceedest the fame that I heard.

Happy *are* thy men, and happy *are* these thy servants, which stand continually before thee, and hear thy wisdom.

Blessed be the Lord thy God, which delighted in thee to set thee on his throne, *to be* king for the Lord thy God: because thy God loved Israel, to establish them for ever, therefore made he thee king over them, to do judgement and justice.

And she gave the king an hundred and twenty talents of gold, and of spices great abundance, and precious stones: neither was there any such spice as the queen of Sheba gave king Solomon.

And the servants also of Huram, and the servants of Solomon, which brought gold from Ophir, brought algum trees and precious stones.

And the king made *of* **the algum trees terraces to the house of the Lord, and to the king's palace, and harps and psalteries for singers: and there were none such seen before in the land of Judah.**

And king Solomon gave to the queen of Sheba all her desire, whatsoever she asked, beside *that* **which she had brought unto the king. So she turned, and went away to her own land, she and her servants.**

II Chronicles 9:1-12

This is a very beautiful story, and I would like you to flow with me as we begin to examine it. Queen Sheba heard of the fame of Solomon and she brought her people to see Solomon. She brought them to get in on his ministry. She brought a host of all of his people, because one thing she had in mind, to embarrass and disgrace Solomon in the midst of his people, to convince his people that he was a dummy. She wanted to destroy the man's ministry. She prepared and sat up all night for questions that she was going to ask Solomon, because she had heard that he was a very wise man. But when she met Solomon, she met a man not only full of wisdom, but a man that walked and flowed in the spirit of excellence.

Christians wonder and complain why we need excellence in our lives and ministries. It is because we want to keep the devil out of our lives and out of our ministries. Don't you want the devil out of your life, out of your job, out of your ministry and out of your family? Then walk in the spirit of excellence and you will knock the devil upside down.

Solomon answered all of the Queen's questions. She came with great authority and power but, because of Solomon's character, there was no more spirit in her. The Living Bible says, **"it took her breath."** Another translation says **"she stagger in all."** This was a woman who came with the purpose of tearing down Solomon's ministry but, because Solomon walked in the spirit of excellence, it diffused her power, took her breath and caused her to stagger in all. She noticed that Solomon's servants and

98

workers were very alert. She noticed the servants apparel. This is a very delicate subject to deal with. Despite the fact that it does not matter how we dress in church or to our services, it is important the way a staff member of a ministry dresses, because he or she is a representative of God and the ministry. God wants us to walk in excellence.

God's Kind of Man

She saw the size of Solomon's men. She saw how happy they were in serving Solomon. She said **"Happy are thy men and happy are these thy servants, which stand continually before thee, and hear thy wisdom."** It does something to the enemy to see men in the Church. It does something to the enemy not to just see men in the Church, but to see men that seem to have good sense, that do not look like they were dragged off the corner of the street. Men that look like they have a good conscience, a life of faith and a fervent spirit. Men that love Jesus and are filled with the Word and power of God — satan hates that. This alarmed Queen Sheba when she came to Solomon's ministry.

Queen Sheba got her plot and scheme prepared. She must have said, "Well, they say he has so much wisdom and riches, I will show him that he is nothing. He will know that I am the Queen of Sheba."

She came only to find no wimps. She came to find men that loved their families, men who were spirit-filled, men who spoke with tongues, loved their leader and men that were dressed finely.

Verse four in the New American Standard Bible version says, "she marvelled at the attendance." She marvelled at the Ministry of Helps. She marvelled at the ushers, she marvelled at the choir and she marvelled at the orchestra.

The Reward for Excellence

Still in the New American Standard version, the Bible says that she lost her breath. Breath is a sign of life and when there is no breath, there is no life. In other words, she lost her life. She was defused.

And she gave the king an hundred and twenty talents of gold, and of spices great abundance, and precious stones: neither was there any such spice as the Queen of Sheba gave king Solomon.

II Chronicles 9:9

The spirit of excellence will make your enemies give to you against their will. Excellence will cause the enemy to realize what he has stolen from you.

And king Solomon gave to the queen of Sheba all her desire, whatsoever she asked, beside *that* which she had brought unto the king. So she turned, and went away to her own land, she and her servants.

II Chronicles 9:12

The spirit of excellence will make the enemy submit, and if the enemy will not submit, the enemy will pack his or her bags and leave. Queen Sheba did not want to submit to Solomon. What she did was to pack her bags and take her things and leave. You don't have to worry about a disgruntled person hanging around you. When you begin to walk in the spirit of excellence, all who will not submit will pack up their bags and belongings and leave.

What Character Is

Now let us go back and actually see what is character. The Greek word for character offers much insight. In the King James version, his

Greek word, **"Character,"** is translated as "image." **"Character,"** is a noun which is derived from the word **"Charasso,"** which means a notch or indentation; a sharpening, scratching or writing on stone, wood or metal. This word came to mean an embosser and a stamp for making coins. From this, it came to mean the embossed stamp made on the coin, or a character styled in writing. This Greek word appears in the New Testament only in Hebrews 1:3. Here, the writer states that Christ is the very character of God, the very stamp of God's nature, and the one in whom God stamped or imprinted His being.

Character not only involves how a person acts, character also includes a person's inner thoughts, motives and attitudes. Thoughts, though hidden, indicate the real character of a person. Motives are true expressions of the inner man. To change the character of a person, one must go deeper than action.

Character is what a person is at this present time. When pressures come upon a person's life, the real person surfaces. A person may act and think one way under the blessings of the Lord, but in quite another way when the trials and heat of life are his portion.

Character is not only that which other people see on the external. Character is what other people do not see. People may see only the side of a person that a person wants to display, but God sees the real person.

Every believer in this Time Zone of the Spirit of God must develop his or her character in these areas — spiritual life, personal life, ministerial life, mental life and financial life.

Excellence, A Key to God's Undivided Attention

It pleased Darius to set over the kingdom an hundred and twenty princes, which should be over the whole kingdom;

101

And over these three presidents; of whom Daniel *was* first: that the princes might give accounts unto them, and the king should have no damage.

Then this Daniel was preferred above the presidents and princes, because an excellent spirit *was* in him; and the king thought to set him over the whole realm.

Daniel 6:1-3

Daniel was a man who walked and operated in the spirit of excellence. He was outstanding and preeminent. He walked so much in excellence that he stood out from the others. Why was Daniel so noticeable from the others? What is it, in some believers today, that makes them stand out from the others? In some churches or ministries, there are some particular Christians that seem to be more prominent than others. The main key to this is because of their "faithfulness to their God." Daniel was faithful to his God and, because of this, he stood out. Because of this, he became prominent. Your faithfulness to God will produce the spirit of excellence.

Then the presidents and princes sought to find occasion against Daniel concerning the kingdom; but they could find none occasion nor fault; forasmuch as he *was* faithful, neither was there any error or fault found in him.

Daniel 6:4

Most men will proclaim every one his own goodness: but a faithful man who can find?

Proverbs 20:6

It is difficult to find faithful believers today. It is difficult to find men and women whose total alliance is to God. That is why the Church is at a crucial time in its history today. God is recruiting not just any kind of people. He is recruiting men and women who will be faithful against any

102

proclamation of Darius. Faithfulness is a virtue that will cause a person to stand out from the crowd and to receive God's undivided attention.

The word, "faithfulness" in the Greek means "trustworthy" or "trustful."

For therein is the righteousness of God revealed from faith to faith: as it is written, the just shall live by faith.

Romans 1:17

Behold, his soul *which* is lifted up is not upright in him: but the just shall live by his faith.

Habakkuk 2:4

In the Hebrew, the word, "faith," in this verse actually means "fairness," "fidelity" or "faithfulness."

Chapter VI

The Restoration of the Kingly Authority and Power

Thou shalt arise, *and* have mercy upon Zion: for the time to favour her, yea, the set time, is come.

For thy servants take pleasure in her stones, and favour the dust thereof.

So the heathen shall fear the name of the Lord, and all the kings of the earth thy glory.

When the Lord shall build up Zion, he shall appear in his glory.

Psalms 102:13-16

In this move of the Spirit of God, the Church will experience a total restoration of both the kingly authority and power, and the worship and service of David's Tabernacle. I believe that now is the "set time" that this will be accomplished. God has promised to favor "Zion," and to restore to her the authority and power which was lost.

The Meaning of Zion

Zion was the place where the Tabernacle of David was pitched, and it was also the place where the king's palace was established. Therefore, whenever the name "Zion" is used in Scripture, it is referring to the pattern of worship, praise and service David established in the Tabernacle of David, as well as the place of kingly power and authority. God has promised to restore David's Tabernacle, to build up Zion and to reveal His glory through Zion.

"Zion" is also a term symbolic of the Church. It symbolizes the people who have the presence and glory of God upon them. It is also a term representative of God's kingly power and the authority of God, which today is flowing through the Church and God's people individually.

Throughout the Old Testament, mountains symbolized kingdoms.

And I will make her that halted a remnant, and her that was cast far off a strong nation: and the Lord shall reign over them in Mount Zion from henceforth, even for ever.

And thou, O tower of the flock, the strong hold of the daughter of Zion, unto thee shall it come, even the first dominion; the kingdom shall come to the daughter of Jerusalem.

Micah 4:7-8

Micah speaks of a time when the Lord shall gather His Church, **"a remnant, and a strong nation and the Lord shall reign over them in Mount Zion ...."** God will restore unto Zion "even the first dominion" ... his might and power and kingly authority. God also promises, through Micah, that the day will come when He will make even those who are weak, lame, and cast down to be a strong and conquering people.

Arise and thresh, O daughter of Zion: for I will make thine horn iron, and I will make thy hoofs brass: and thou shalt beat in pieces many people: and I will consecrate their gain unto the Lord, and their substance unto the Lord of the whole earth.

Micah 4:13

It is even much clearer here, for God tells His people to **"arise and thresh"** as He makes their horn iron and their hoofs brass. The iron horn and brass hoofs symbolize the power of God's people to thresh down and tread the enemy underfoot.

And thou, O tower of the flock, the strong hold of the daughter of Zion, unto thee shall it come, even the first dominion; the kingdom shall come to the daughter of Jerusalem.

Micah 4:8

Micah also speaks of the stronghold of the daughter of Zion being the tower of the flock. Under David, there was a tower on Mount Zion to which David and his mighty men would return after a battle. There, they would take off their bucklers and shields, and hang them up in the tower. This they did as a sign that the battle was over, and the victory was won.

Thy neck *is* like the tower of David builded for an armoury, whereon there hang a thousand bucklers, all shields of mighty men.

Song of Solomon 4:4

Solomon wrote prophetically about the strong tower on Mount Zion. He describes the bride to represent her. This speaks to us, today, of the Bride of Christ, the Church, for whom the battle is over.

The Church, the believers of the new covenant of faith and the grace are the inheritors of the promises God gave regarding Zion. We are the spiritual Zion, being built up by the Lord to contain His glory.

The Glory of God

The Hebrew word for "glory" is "kabod." It comes from a root word which means "a heavy weight."

For our light affliction, which is but for a moment, worketh for us a far more exceeding *and* **eternal weight of glory.**

II Corinthians 4:17

The Apostle Paul spoke of the "glory" as an "eternal weight of glory." With the "heavy weight" of the glory comes the "heavy weight" of responsibility which believers, as New Testament priests, must be prepared to bear in this Time Zone.

I am convinced that, in these, the last days, we are going to see such an increase in the power of our worship and in the glory of God, that even those with great power and authority, if they are not a part of spiritual Zion, are going to fear God's glory. We are going to see the heathens of the earth fearing the name of the Lord, and the rulers of the earth His glory.

Matured Priesthood

Beyond learning to be responsible in our service, God is calling His people to a mature priesthood. We need to come before Him with purity, holiness and reverence.

Purity

As we worship in the Tabernacle of David, standing before the presence of God, we must come in purity with clean garments, prepared to minister unto Him. God is again restoring those who have been in captivity, whose lives have been torn apart, who have been in the enemy's hands. He is bringing them to the house of healing, and is healing their bruises and their tearing. He is restoring them to Himself, and making them durable, loving and kind. He is making the qualities of the Holy Spirit become more and more evident within their lives.

As He restores, He is making His people responsible for bearing His glory, as well.

All around the world, God is speaking about the need to wait upon the Lord, so that His light can search our hearts and reveal anything that prevents us from ministering properly to Him, with pure hearts and clean hands.

Holiness

As we work to develop a pure heart, there is a need to measure ourselves by God's standard of holiness.

And the Jews' passover was at hand, and Jesus went up to Jerusalem.

John 2:13

Jesus came into this setting unwilling to compromise the standard of God's Word. He drove out those who had made His Father's house a den of thieves, and He did not back down when He was opposed.

Thou son of man, show the house to the house of Israel, that they may be ashamed of their iniquities: and let them measure the pattern.

And if they be ashamed of all that they have done, show them the form of the house, and the fashion thereof, and the goings out thereof, and the comings in thereof, and all forms thereof, and all the ordinances thereof, and all forms thereof, and all the laws thereof: and write *it* **in their sight, that they may keep the whole form thereof, and all the ordinances thereof, and do them.**

This *is* **the law of the house; Upon the top of the mountain the whole limit thereof round about** *shall be* **most holy. Behold, this** *is* **the law of the house.**

Ezekiel 43:10-12

Here the Scripture tells us that there is a law of the house of God by which His house shall be measured. What is the law of the house? **"Upon the top of the mountain the whole limit thereof round about shall be most Holy."** Let us measure ourselves according to the standard of holiness, to allow God to reveal His glory in our lives.

> **Rise, and measure the temple of God, and the altar, and them that worship therein.**
>
> **Revelation 11:1b**

Let us **"Rise, and measure the temple of God ... and them that worship therein,"** for if we fail to do so, God will Himself measure us, and may find us wanting.

We have a divine, heavy weight of responsibility to be a pure and holy priesthood before the Lord. When we fall short of that responsibility, we are making the Father's house into something that fails to meet His standard, so that it no longer can be the house of the Lord. His living glory departs, and over the door He writes, "Ichabod, the glory has departed."

Reverence

We need to maintain an attitude of reverence and awe in the presence of the Lord.

> **In the year that king Uzziah died I saw also the Lord sitting upon a throne, high and lifted up, and his train filled the temple.**
>
> **Isaiah 6:1**

Isaiah's vision took place "in the year that king Uzziah died ...." King Uzziah was a king of Judah who increased the military strength of Judah.

But when he was strong, his heart was lifted up to *his* **destruction: for he transgressed against the Lord his God, and went into the temple of the Lord to burn incense upon the altar of incense.**

And Azariah the priest went in after him, and with him fourscore priests of the Lord, *that were* **valiant men:**

And they withstood Uzziah the king, and said unto him, *It appertaineth* **not unto thee, Uzziah, to burn incense unto the Lord, but the priests the sons of Aaron, that are consecrated to burn incense: go out of the sanctuary; for thou has trespassed; neither** *shall it be* **for thine honour from the Lord God.**

Then Uzziah was wroth, and *had* **a censer in his hand to burn incense: and while he was wroth with the priests, the leprosy even rose up in his forehead before the priests in the house of the Lord; from beside the incense altar.**

An Azariah the chief priest, and all the priests, looked upon him, and, behold, he *was* **leprous in his forehead, and they thrust him out from thence; yea, himself hasted also to go out, because the Lord had smitten him.**

And Uzziah the king was a leper unto the day of his death, and dwelt in a several house, *being* **a leper; for he was cut off from the house of the Lord: and Jotham his son** *was* **over the king's house, judging the people of the land.**

II Chronicles 26:16-21

Because of his carelessness and presumption, God judged Uzziah and he became a leper, cut off from God's house. Uzziah's judgement had given Isaiah a very vivid picture of the holiness of God, and he was better able to recognize his own unworthiness to stand in God's presence, because of his own sin.

There was a need for cleansing and the purging of sin in his life, and until that took place, Isaiah was in danger of judgement.

As he stood there in fear, God made provision for his need and removed his iniquity, purging his sin from him by the coal from the altar. God is, today, doing a purging work in His people, preparing us to be sent out on His behalf.

The Rain and Shower

Ask ye of the Lord rain in the time of the latter rain, so the Lord shall make bright clouds, and give them showers of rain, to every one grass in the field.

Zechariah 10:1

The rain is about to fall in this Time Zone. The showers are about to hit the Church in this hour. This rain and shower that the Church will experience will cleanse the Body of Christ from any form of spiritual poison and contamination that has flowed in its veins. Rain can be uncomfortable at times, but we need it for a refreshing and for the harvest of God.

The Enthroning and Dethroning

And he changeth the times and the seasons: he removeth kings, and setteth up kings: he giveth wisdom unto the wise, and knowledge to them that know understanding.

Daniel 2:21

Just like as of old, when God set up kings and disposed of them, I strongly believe that in this Time Zone, the Body of Christ will experience the raising up of many unknown ministries, churches and leaders to declare the known — the Word of the Lord and will see the disposing of many known and great ministries. These ministries will not be taken off of the scene, but their role will be decreased and minimized.

Sleeping Leaders

And Jacob awaked out of his sleep, and he said, Surely the Lord is in this place; and I knew it not.

Genesis 28:16

Just like Jacob, many leaders and Christians of great ministries and churches are still sleeping through the visitation of the Holy Spirit, only to wake up and realize that "surely the Lord is in this place, and I was not aware of it." They are not aware because they have been sleeping all night, pretending that they are seeking the Lord.

No Prophet, No Rain

And Elijah the Tishbite, who was of the inhabitants of Gilead, said unto Ahab, As the Lord God of Israel liveth, before whom I stand, there shall not be dew nor rain these years, but according to my word.

I Kings 17:1

The Body of Christ, in this Time Zone, must realize quickly the role and the need of the prophetic anointing and mantle on our lives and land. This is not to lift up one ministry gift higher than another, because the five-fold ministry gifts are needed today. But we must realize that God, in this hour, has chosen the office of the prophet and apostle to pioneer this prophetic move, even though all of the other five-fold ministry gifts will walk under this mantle. Churches, ministries and our land will not experience in full propensity the movement of the Holy Spirit — the rain and the dew - until the prophetic words that are spoken by true prophets today are adhered to. I am not talking about false prophets. I am talking about those who have been called and ordained by God to the prophetic office. Just like the prophet Elijah said, there will be no rain nor dew except at his word. The prophets that are called, those God is raising up in this Time Zone, will stand with boldness and declare the righteousness of God and the arrival of the rain of the Holy Spirit.

The Place of "Cutting Away"

And the word of the Lord came unto him, saying,

Get thee hence, and turn thee eastward, and hide thyself by the brook Cherith, that is before Jordan.

And it shall be, that thou shalt drink of the brook; and I have commanded the ravens to feed thee there.

I Kings 17:2-4

"Cherith" means "a cutting away." The Lord instructed Elijah to go to Cherith and there He would send the ravens to feed him. Cherith is the place of readiness and preparation for our lives. It is the place where certain things of our flesh need to be cut away. Without these things being cut away, we can not get to Zarephath. Notice what Elijah was to be supplied with — water and meat. The water represents the anointing and the meat represents the Word. This is where it is developed, at Cherith — the place of readiness. Have you visited your brook Cherith, or are you still in the land of Israel, where famine and drought has been declared? This is a question you need to ask yourself before continuing to read the remainder of this book. Interestingly, you, your church or ministry and your leader might still be living and building your tents in a move that is experiencing famine and drought.

I hear God saying this to the Church today, "Find that brook of Cherith and run quickly to it, for in it you will find water (the anointing) and meat (the Word of the Lord)." After the "cutting away" process,

Elijah was then able to move to "Zarephath" where his call, ministry, and anointing would be refined, defined and blossom.

The Place Called Zarephath
for the Church of the 90s

And it came to pass after a while, that the brook dried up, because there had been no rain in the land.

And the word of the Lord came unto him, saying,

Arise, get thee to Zarephath, which *belongeth* **to Zidon, and dwell there: behold, I have commanded a widow woman there to sustain thee.**

I Kings 17:7-9

Zarephath, for God's people in this hour, will be the place of refinement, development and launching ground. It will be a place where many calls, anointings and ministries will be defined. As long as there is water in the "brook Cherith" of your ministry and church, stay there, do not leave or move. But once you know that the brook has dried up, get out of there quickly. Do not let anyone convince you to remain. Many churches, ministries and Christians all over the world are still building projects, calls, churches and ministries in brooks that have dried up.

This is one reason why churches are dried up today. There is no water (anointing) and there is no meat (the Word of the Lord) to sustain God's people in these places. "Many," says the Lord, "will hear the Word of the Lord while in these dry brooks (churches, ministries and organizations) to move to 'Zarephath — place of fiery furnace' and in Zarephath, these individuals will develop, cherish and understand their calling." Their ministry and anointing will be properly defined. As long as you are in a dry brook, everything about you will be dry — especially your anointing.

115

The Word of the Lord will become scarce, rare and precious in your life, church and ministry.

All that Glitters are no More Gold

The earth shall quake before them; the heavens shall tremble: the sun and the moon shall be dark, and the stars shall withdraw their shining.

Joel 2:10

The glittering ministries and churches are gradually fading away. You do not have to be a rocket scientist to discern this. It is real, and it will become more real in this new Time Zone of the Spirit of God. The superstars are no longer shining. God is raising up men and women to go to "Zarephath in Zidon."

Listen carefully, there is something about the location of "Zarephath." It is located in "Zidon," which means a "hunting place." In other words, the place of "refinement" is located in a "hunting place." This means that, in order to get to the place of refinement (Zarephath), we have to become hunters. We have to hunt for God and His attributes, and not those of the Christian superstars. Remember, these superstars are fading away. But God, our great Creator, will remain forevermore!

Having A Continual Ministry

As David appointed singers to worship and praise God in the Tabernacle, he ensured that their ministry continued around the clock. He appointed different choruses who were responsible for ministering at different times throughout the day and night.

God wants us, as New Testament priests, to have a continual ministry unto Him, according to the worship of the Tabernacle of David.

I will bless the Lord at all times: his praise *shall* continually *be* in my mouth.

Psalms 34:1

Surely goodness and mercy shall follow me all the days of my life: and I will dwell in the house of the Lord forever.

Psalms 23:6

We are not to minister only when we feel like it, but regularly, consistently and continually. If we don't feel like it, we should still worship Him anyway, because He is worthy of our worship.

As believers of the new covenant of faith and grace, we must have the desire in our heart to be responsible and mature priests, ministering continually before the Lord. We must learn to treat our calling to be king and priests before the Lord as not only a privilege, but also as an awesome responsibility.

No matter what our ministry, we must be faithful at our place of ministry, considering ourselves to be under an obligation to the Lord in our service. We are to treat every opportunity to worship and to serve Him as a divine appointment.

Chapter VII

The Restoration of God's Prophetic Anointing

God is restoring, in full, the prophetic anointing to the Church today. This prophetic anointing is for those of God's people who have a desire to flow in the rivers of God, but just cannot find their ways out of the well. This anointing is for those who cannot seem to bear the fruit of the Spirit in their seasons, because they are not planted by the streams of living water.

He turneth rivers into a wilderness, and the watersprings into dry ground

And there he maketh the hungry to dwell, that they may prepare a city for habitation.

Psalms 107:33,36

The flow of this prophetic anointing will establish us and make us a city inhabited by God, Himself.

Look upon Zion, the city of our solemnities: thine eyes shall see Jerusalem a quiet habitation, a tabernacle *that* **shall not be taken down; not one of the stakes thereof shall ever be removed, neither shall any of the cords thereof be broken.**

But there the glorious Lord *will be* **unto us a place of broad rivers** *and* **streams; wherein shall go no galley with oars, neither shall gallant ship pass thereby.**

Isaiah 33:20-21

In the past movement of God, tradition has caused the Body of Christ to jump into the water and try to flow with oars of the flesh; and in the sight of man, most believers have become mighty ships. But, as God says, no boats or ships can flow in this river.

What is the Prophetic Anointing?

He sendeth forth his commandment *upon* earth: his word runneth very swiftly.

Psalms 147:15

What does it mean to be prophetic? God's wind is blowing upon the land again. God blows upon the Church according to His own will, according to His own sovereignty. The winds of God are blowing His prophetic anointing upon the Church now. This anointing is one that makes a child of God hear more expressly and explicitly from God, and makes them walk in godly wisdom above and beyond the natural realm.

This prophetic anointing gives the saints of God a confidence and assurance that when God speaks, you know it is He speaking. He can come in a still, small voice or a rumbling earthquake, but whatever His mode or revelation to you is, because of this anointing, you know that it is God! God is desiring a prophetic people in this hour.

The word "prophetic" is an adjective that describes the prophets of God. These prophets of God will be men and women called by God, Himself, to a ministry of confrontation. They will be proclaimers of God's Word to the people. They will stay in a position to hear from God, and intimacy will be one of the main characteristics of their ministry gift. Not only will God speak to them about their own actions, but God will give prophetic words to His prophets to proclaim according to His direction.

These prophets will be praying men and women who know how to hold on to the horns of the altar and bring down the strongholds of satan's kingdom. God will use these instruments to provoke His people to a realm of holiness and ultimate blessings as a result of their obedience. They will speak the Word of the Lord, which will give the people of God clarity of the present and of the future. The words they will speak will always reveal God's purpose in any given situation.

When the nation of Israel found themselves in many valleys, it was the prophet who spoke the Word of the Lord, and that anointing was able to bring the people of God back to the mountain top.

Now don't get me wrong, just as I've said in the previous chapters, God is not calling the Church, as a whole, to become prophets. God is calling the Body of Christ to become a prophetic people. By becoming a prophetic people, we take on the characteristics of the prophet. Not only will this anointing restore the full awareness and respect of the prophets within the Body, but it will bring those characteristics upon the Church corporately. For instance, another characteristic of the prophet of God is the ability to prophesy.

Follow after charity, and desire spiritual *gifts*, but rather that ye may prophesy.

I Corinthians 14:1

We can see that God wants us to have an earnest desire to prophesy. And since this one characteristic of the prophet is explicitly introduced to the Church as a whole, then we can set our hearts to be zealous, diligent, eager, fervent and overly anxious about desiring the prophetic today.

And Moses went out, and told the people the words of the Lord, and gathered the seventy men of the elders of the people, and set them round about the tabernacle.

121

And the Lord came down in a cloud, and spake unto him, and took of the spirit that *was* upon him, and gave *it* unto the seventy elders: and it came to pass, *that*, when the spirit rested upon them, they prophesied, and did not cease.

But there remained two *of the* men in the camp, the name of the one *was* Eldad, and the name of the other Medad: and the spirit rested upon them; and they *were* of them that were written, but went not out unto the tabernacle: and they prophesied in the camp.

And there ran a young man, and told Moses, and said, Eldad and Medad do prophesy in the camp.

And Joshua the son of Nun, the servant of Moses, *one* of his young men, answered and said, My lord Moses, forbid them.

And Moses said unto him, Enviest thou for my sake? Would God that all the Lord's people were prophets, *and* that the Lord would put his spirit upon them!

Numbers 11:24-29

We see that it is God's desire that all of the Lord's people would know how to flow in this prophetic anointing. It has to do with God pouring out His Spirit upon His people. This is the time and hour of the prophetic anointing. This is the instrument that God will use today to bring about a prepared people. This is the instrument that God will use to manifest His power among the people.

So many Christians do not know how to hear from God. They do not know how to listen to God. They do not know which direction to take, because the guidance from the Holy Spirit is foreign to them. We say "every hair on my head is numbered, so God really cares about me," but when we come to that fork in the road (who to marry, what church to go to, what ministry am I called to), we all go forward with our own understanding, without first discovering what God wants us to do. This

122

prophetic anointing that God is pouring out in this hour will enable the Body of Christ to pinpoint accurately the wisdom that should be manifested in the lives of God's people, and also reveal itself through willing vessels or instruments to bring that wisdom and knowledge to those who need it around us. There are those within the Body of Christ that are unsure and do not have confidence or assurance when God speaks; but because of this anointing that God is pouring out in this hour, the potential to hear from God is now greater.

We all have a part to play in this prophetic move. Because the awareness and actuality of the ministry of the prophet is being restored, it will produce a "domino effect" on the other ministry gifts in becoming prophetic. We will see the ministry gift of the teacher, apostle, pastor and evangelist being prophetic in this hour.

They will speak continually from the presence of God. Their offices, will be so connected with heaven that every single word they say will be as if God is talking in person. Because of the accuracy of their words, many will think these ministry gifts are prophets and will start calling these individuals prophets. They are not prophets. They are those who have yielded themselves under the mantle or umbrella of this prophetic anointing that God has poured in the land. And the reason they are flowing like they are is because they have embraced the prophetic anointing and began to operate in certain characteristics of the prophets.

Prior Prophets versus Now Prophets

God wants all of His people to be prophetic and not all of His people being prophets. Let me draw a distinction here between those that were used in this office prior to God's prophetic movement now. You might say, "God called me to be a prophet back in the 70s," or "I have been operating in the gifts of the Spirit before this prophetic movement came upon the scene," or "I have been giving personal prophecy to people for years now." Well, this is the distinction. God chooses certain instruments for certain seasons that He has ordained for the Church. Let me bring it home. If you were operating as a prophet before this Time Zone, there is now more power under this umbrella to fulfill God's purpose.

For instance, in the 40s, 50s and 60s (like I said in the previous chapter), God was using the evangelist as the instrument during that season. The anointing on the ministry gift of the evangelist produced gifts of healings and miracles, causing massive conversion to Christ. You might have been one who was called to be a pastor at the same time. You were operating in the ministry gift of a pastor but it was the instrument of the evangelist that was chosen in that particular season. It was the evangelistic anointing that God was pouring out at that time. This did not negate apostles, prophets, pastors, and those called to teach. Now is the time of the anointing of the prophet. (The accompanying characteristics making God's people prophetic.)

In the past, because of the lack of acknowledgment and honor for the ministry gift of the prophet, God's purposes could not be fulfilled in great magnitude, for the restoration of this office had not come to the fullness of time. But in the fullness of time, God is now providing His Church the revelation of the prophetic ministries.

This prophetic anointing is hovering over the land, and in order to walk in it, you must place yourself underneath it.

Prophetic Presbytery

Not only is God calling prophets forth in the land today; or having those called to the other ministry gifts to move in the prophetic or having even the layman manifest some characteristics of this anointing; there will

124

also be prophetic presbytery. This will consist of seasonal prophetic ministers who will have one purpose in mind, and that is to prophesy the Word of the Lord to you regarding your life. God will use this presbytery to stir up, confirm and strengthen the gifts that He has given to the Body of Christ.

Activating the Gifts of the Spirit

In the past, we have had so much teaching on the gifts of the Spirit that I think we are about to burst out with knowledge if any more comes our way. We know about the nine gifts, we know the meaning of all the gifts, we can quote Scriptures in locating the manifestations of these gifts in the Bible, but we have not moved out in manifesting them ourselves.

The prophetic anointing will activate the gifts of the Spirit in the Body of Christ. You cannot learn how to operate any particular gift if you do not even know what gift you have. This move of God will reveal to the saints what gifts reside inside of them.

Worship and Song

The prophetic anointing will also manifest itself in our worship and song. It will cause the Body of Christ to be more in tune to how God would want us to approach His throne.

Our songs will change, for they will be songs that cannot and will not be rehearsed. The spontaneity of the Spirit will cause those who walk in faith to sing new songs. This anointing will move upon our music, and those with ears to hear will tell the difference. The Old Testament bears witness to those who know how to prophesy with their instruments, and in this hour, we will begin to see greater manifestations of prophetic music.

Chapter VIII

The Time for Spiritual Division of Labor

But unto every one of us is given grace according to the measure of the gift of Christ.

Wherefore he saith, When he ascended up on high, he led captivity captive, and gave gifts unto men.

Now that he ascended, what is it but that he also descended first into the lower parts of the earth?

He that descended is the same also that ascended up far above all heavens, that he might fill all things.

And he gave some, apostles; and some, prophets; and some, evangelists; and some, pastor and teachers;

For the perfecting of the saints, for the work of the ministry, for the edifying of the body of Christ.

Ephesians 4:7-12

The Church, in this hour, will experience spiritual division of labor. For long, the Body of Christ has operated as a "Jack-of-all-trades and master of none." As a result of this, the Body of Christ has failed to fully maximize the potential of God within them. I believe that the Spirit of God, in this hour, will cause the spirit of division of labor and specialization to rest upon the Church.

We will see specialization of anointings among the churches, among ministry gifts, and among cities and states. The Spirit of God will create in ministry gifts specialization that they never knew they had. The Body of Christ will see apostles, prophets, teachers, evangelists and pastors specializing in various areas of anointing in this hour. These individuals, as never before, will be known and recognized for their specialties. All of these will not come by man's choice of specialty, but it will be by the Spirit of God.

Ministers, for long, have jumped from one office and calling to another because of financial reasons. Everybody wants to become an evangelist for the purpose of raising money, when God actually did not call them to that office. We have those who will do anything to call themselves prophets and apostles, when God actually has not called them.

This is the predicament of the Church today. Because of this jumping, the Body of Christ has not been perfected (matured), equipped for ministry and edified (built up). The Church has gone lacking in certain areas, because men and women who were called to fulfill certain roles and functions have abandoned their calls, offices and gifts for something else. This is why God, through His Spirit, is restoring back to His Church the spirit of division of labor and specialization. This specialization will be obvious in the lives of many ministers, their ministries and their churches, and the Body of Christ will be perfected, equipped and edified again.

What Is Spiritual Division of Labor?

Spiritual division of labor is the specialization by believers in areas of their callings, anointings and gifts, without assuming the responsibilities of another's office.

A good example of spiritual division of labor can be beautifully illustrated from the business of producing straight pins. The production of pins is divided into about eighteen distinct operations. In division of labor, one man or two men cannot perform these tasks of operation alone. It would be tiresome and tedious.

A workman not educated in this business could perhaps make one pin in a day, but certainly not twenty. But with division of labor in operation, one man draws out the wire, another straightens it, a third cuts it, a fourth points it, and a fifth grinds it at the top for receiving the head. The making of the head requires two or three distinct operations; to put it on is a different business in itself, to whiten the pins is another. It is even a trade by itself to put them into the paper, and the important business of making a pin is, in this manner divided into about eighteen distinct operations. Only with division of labor would this be accomplished in a much shorter time.

The Body of Christ

For the body is not one member, but many.

If the foot shall say, Because I am not the hand, I am not of the body; is it therefore not of the body?

And if the ear shall say, Because I am not the eye, I am not of the body; is it therefore not of the body?

If the whole body *were* an eye, where *were* the hearing? If the whole *were* hearing, where *were* the smelling?

But now hath God set the members every one of them in the body, as it hath pleased him.

And if they were all one member, where *were* the body?

But now *are they* **many members, yet but one body.**

And the eye cannot say unto the hand, I have no need of thee: nor again the head to the feet, I have no need of you.

Nay, much more those members of the body, which seem to be more feeble, are necessary:

And those *members* **of the body, which we think to be less honourable, upon these we bestow more abundant honour; and our uncomely** *parts* **have more abundant comeliness.**

That there should be no schism in the body; but *that* **the members should have the same care for another.**

I Corinthians 12:14-23,25

The same applies to the Body of Christ. God is calling for spiritual division of labor. He is calling for specialization. There is no time for competition. The final products that will be produced in this hour will be a full contribution of the entire Body of Christ.

The eye is a contributor, the nose, the ear, the foot and the hands are all contributors to the body. The ear cannot say because he is not the eye, that he is not a part of the body, nor can the eye say that because he is not the ear, he is not a part of the body. This is the problem that the Body of Christ has been undergoing for a long time. Because of our desire to be in the limelight, we refuse to consider the importance of certain calls, gifts and offices. If it is not one of those prominent ministry gifts, we do not accept them. However, God is doing something new. He is causing believers and leaders to embrace the spirit of division of labor.

What Is Specialization?

The birds that fly do it. The bees that sting do it. What do they do? They specialize. Specialization is the division of productive activities among individuals and regions, so that no one person or region is self-sufficient.

The Results of Specialization

The result of spiritual division of labor and specialization brings enormous gain to the Body of Christ, because each individual is able to use the gift of God upon his life to the best advantage of the Body of Christ.

Spiritual division of labor and specialization will create and produce four vital ingredients for the Body of Christ.

- It will allow the development and the refinement of the call, gift, skill and anointing upon the lives of God's people.

- It will help the Body of Christ to avoid the wasted time of jumping from one call or office to another.

- It will cause believers to refocus on what God has called them to do.

- It will enable believers, leaders and churches to fully maximize their potentials and to give more than they receive. This will then make it necessary for believers to share with one another, without the thought of competition because one has what the other does not have. So we need one another to benefit from what the other has.

Areas of Specialization

Specialization will be demonstrated in three vital areas in this Time Zone.

The first area will be the specialization of ministry gifts — apostles, prophets, evangelists, pastors and teachers.

The second area will be the specialization among churches.

The final area will be specialization of cities, states and countries.

Each area will display a unique anointing that will stand out and be recognizable as a characteristic of the individual entity. Each area's specialty will be obvious to others and characterized by its quality.

Specialization of Ministry Gifts

Not only has God raised up and set the five-fold ministry gifts in the Church today, but in this hour, specialization will be birthed from within each of these ministry gifts. These specializations will be created to accomplish very specific purposes and callings that have been neglected within the Body of Christ. It is already happening. The Body of Christ, in this Time Zone, will witness the rapid growth of these specialized ministries. They will not come with a general message, but they will appear on God's map with specific and accurate messages for the Church. They will come with the "NOW" messages.

They will walk and flow in the realm of grace meant for that anointing. They will walk in the calling with all boldness and confidence. This is spiritual division of labor. Believers will become specialists in the areas that God has called them to. Ministers, for many years, have tried to be a jack-of-all-trades and they end up being a master of none. We do so much, and yet, the anointing is not there to aid our assignment. The anointing will appear when you abide in your calling and take it very serious. The anointing will not appear if you are in someone else's vineyard.

There are apostles that God is raising up in this hour that will specialize in certain areas within the apostolic calling. This has always been a difficult office to come to, because of the criticism that has been associated with false apostles. Criticism or no criticism, God, in this hour, is raising up true leaders with the apostolic anointing upon their lives. They are appearing everywhere. These individuals will possess certain specific assignments that will become a trademark of their calling. We will see apostles whose sole specialty will be on deliverance. We will see apostles of intercessions, apostles of war, and we will see those with the anointing to tear down and rebuild broken walls and burnt cities. As these leaders appear on the scene, the Church has a responsibility to receive them and honor their callings, anointings and specialties. They have been released into the earth, and they have a specific purpose and anointing in this hour.

Not only with apostles will the Church see specialization. There will be specialties also among true prophets. These groups of specialized prophets are already hitting the beach of our hearts, churches and ministries. We will see specialties with prophets in the areas of deliverance, intercession and predictions. We will see those prophets who just specialize in prophesying the Word. There will be prophets of war, prophets of restoration and revival, and these prophets will blow the trumpets concerning the move of God from the specialty anointing on their offices. As a result of these specialties coming to the Church, the Body of Christ will hear the constant repetition of certain messages from these men. Don't be bored. Don't run from their meetings. Listen to them! It is because the anointing of God is upon their lives to stand in that specialization. We will witness specialization among evangelists, pastors and teachers. We will see these ministry gifts flow in the specialty, with no form of competition and with great confidence.

Specialization of Ministries

And beside this, giving all diligence, add to your faith virtue; and to virtue knowledge;

And to knowledge temperance; and to temperance patience; and to patience godliness;

And to godliness brotherly kindness; and to brotherly kindness charity.

For if these things be in you, and abound, they make *you that ye shall* neither *be* barren nor unfruitful in the knowledge of our Lord Jesus Christ.

But he that lacketh these things is blind, and cannot see afar off, and hath forgotten that he was purged from his old sins.

Wherefore the rather, brethren, give diligence to make your calling and election sure: for if ye do these things, ye shall never fall:

For so an entrance shall be ministered unto you abundantly into the everlasting kingdom of our Lord and Savior Jesus Christ.

II Peter 1:5-11

Just like the specialized ministry gifts, God, through His Spirit, is causing ministries and churches to specialize in certain areas. These specialized ministries and churches will be known by the unique "sound" that they produce. It will be so unique that it will declare and show the specialization of that ministry. We will experience, see and hear ministries that will be known for their great emphasis on holiness, on deliverance, on prosperity, on intercessory prayer and on restoration. Some will greatly re-emphasize the office of the prophet. There will be churches that are prophetically inclined, evangelically inclined, apostolically inclined and others will be purely teaching ministries. All is needed within the Body of Christ. In addition, these ministries and churches will preach and minister on other areas of the Word of God. But their strong specialty will be what they re-emphasize often. The reason for this is because the anointing of God is upon them for that specialty.

Keys to Ministry Specialization

Two vital keys will cause a ministry or church to operate from the specialized calling and anointing.

The first key is that every church and ministry must learn the original anointing of his or her establishment. When this is found and understood, the leadership of this house must steer the ship of his vision and congregation towards that anointing. Many times, Christians don't understand why that is needed. One of the key reasons is because that is the place of your calling. As churches and ministries begin to operate, walk and build upon their callings, it will become easy to appreciate one another without being envious or critical. As ministries and churches become obedient toward their specialized anointings, God will begin to add more specialties to them. This reminds me of Dr. Lester Sumrall's ministry. Even though he ministers in other areas of the world, his strong emphasis and specialization is on deliverance. The same applies to Apostle Ernest Leonard, Oral Roberts, Benny Hinn, Prophet Bernard Jordan, Dr. John Avanzini, Kenneth Hagin and a host of others. Their ministering lies in their specializations. One ministers and emphasizes restoration, while another ministers healing. Another specializes in teaching finance and the other specializes in delivering the Word of the Lord. Isn't it beautiful?

This is spiritual division of labor. Everyone participates to achieve one common goal.

The second key is after finding and locating the calling or anointing upon that church or ministry, that anointing must be properly developed by diligence, and refocusing the members of the ministry toward the original purpose and call on the ministry. Many leaders have churches today who do not know the calling, anointing and assignment on the ministry. The lack of this has caused many to take upon their ministry and church the assignment, call, purpose and anointing of other ministries and churches. I pray that after reading this book, you will ask yourself this provoking question — "What is the assignment, call, anointing and purpose of my ministry or church?" As Brother Myles Monroe said, "If you don't know the purpose of a thing, you will abuse that thing." You can abuse the anointing if you don't know its purpose on your ministry or church.

Specialization of Cities

Because of specialization in the ministry gifts and on the Church, there will be specialization among cities and states. Cities and states will be known in this hour to specialize in certain areas of God's anointing. We will hear of cities that are more prophetic than others. Just as Tulsa, Oklahoma is known for the "Word Revival" and Word of Faith folks, there will be cities and states that will also be known for their emphasis on the prophetic anointing, the deliverance anointing, the restoration message, the intercessory anointing and the apostolic anointing. Some will be known for their teaching and evangelistical anointing. Christians will travel far and near to attend meetings in these cities and states, and when they leave, they will leave blessed and touched, because they have encountered a specialized anointing in that city or state.

The true revelation of the purpose of the Church is unfolding. The Church will be established in this hour.

Grace to Accomplish Assignments

Let's look again at these Scriptures:

But unto every one of us is given grace according to the measure of the gift of Christ.

Wherefore he saith, When he ascended up on high, he led captivity captive, and gave gifts unto men.

Now that he ascended, what is it but that he also descended first into the lower parts of the earth?

He that descended is the same also that ascended up far above all heavens, that he might fill all things.

And he gave some, apostles; and some, prophets; and some, evangelists; and some, pastors and teachers;

For the perfecting of the saints, for the work of the ministry, for the edifying of the body of Christ.

Ephesians 4:7-12

Grace is given in direct proportion to the gift of God upon our lives. The Scripture says, here, that everyone of us is given this grace. When the Word of God says everyone, it means everyone, you and I included. We have been given grace according to the measure of the gift of Christ. In verse 11, the Scripture begins to show us the various gifts that God has given to the Church. These gifts are accompanied by corresponding grace. "He gave some apostles, some prophets, some evangelists, some pastors and teachers." Among these ministry gifts will emanate other specialties in this hour.

> For I say, through the grace given unto me, to every man that is among you, not to think *of himself* more highly than he ought to think; but to think soberly, according as God hath dealt to every man the measure of faith.
>
> For as we have many members in one body, and all members have not the same office:
>
> So we, *being* many, are one body in Christ, and every one members one of another.
>
> Having then gifts differing according to the grace that is given to us, whether prophecy, *let us prophesy* according to the proportion of faith;
>
> Or ministry, *let us wait* on *our* ministering: or he that teacheth, on teaching;
>
> Or he that exhorteth, on exhortation: he that giveth, *let him do it* with simplicity; he that ruleth, with diligence; he that showeth mercy; with cheerfulness.

Romans 12:3-8

Again, in this Scripture, we begin to see that there is certain grace that accompanies the gifts that God has set in the Church. In other words, if God calls a believer to the office of a pastor, there will be grace upon the life of that individual to fulfill the will of God. The same applies to the apostles and the prophets. There will be a supernatural enabling that will give the individual of that office and call the power to fulfill God's assignment.

Spiritual Intruders

We have many spiritual intruders within the Body of Christ today. We have men and women who will not abide in their callings. They are never satisfied with their callings. They are always looking for other callings and offices with "greener pastures." Their purposes are self-motivated and self-oriented. These individuals are "intruders." They intrude in other people's callings and offices. One day they are pastors, another day they are teachers, then evangelists, prophets and apostles. One day they are called and another day they are not called. They have no foundation. They are not stable. Many hop from one call to the other because of financial gain or popularity. They are always changing like the chameleon. If the office of the teacher or pastor is the most popular, they will immediately tag themselves a teacher or a pastor, and vice versa with other ministry gifts.

Spiritual intruders are individuals within the Body of Christ who unlawfully enter into the lands (offices, callings and ministries) and tenements owned by another without permission or welcome. They are individuals who force on themselves callings and offices without God's approval. They are around today. Watch out for these intruders. They may even be in your church and ministries.

It is a dangerous thing to operate in another man's calling and office. Many have taken over positions that belong to others without God's permission and approval. As you read this book, examine and ask yourself if that office, calling and gifts upon your life actually has God's stamp of approval and permission upon it, or did you just move into it because you see and hear someone else doing it; or because someone told you that you are that; or did you inherit the position because of the virtue of your parents' position? These are "food-for-thought" questions. God is not playing in this hour. Spiritual intruders, in this hour, will be exposed and put down. Every Christian leader, minister and church that will operate in this new Time Zone must have the approval of the Spirit of God. I am not talking about approval from man or friends, but a stamp of approval from the throne of God. That is the only way that we will remain untouchable from the devices and schemes of the enemy.

It is very important that we abide and remain in our calling and office. Remaining in your calling and office will produce the corresponding grace and favor which, in turn, produces the needed essential lubrication and the flow with less, or no, resistance and effort. But when you are abiding in another man's calling, you will lack the lubrication and flow. You will look and sound rusty. The problem with most Christians, and surprisingly, leaders today, is that they do not even know what their callings are. It is not, therefore, surprising that they fly like butterflies from one calling, office, church and ministry to another.

When you intrude into an office without God's calling upon your life, you will not experience the benefits of the true gift that has been deposited within you, because grace will only cover the position God has set you in. Grace is not a powerless ingredient, and neither is it an opportunity for undisciplined lifestyles. Once you have found out what your calling is, then take advantage of the grace that has been made available to you in that call or office.

Chapter IX

The Danger of Not Embracing
God's Time Zone

And Rehoboam went to Shechem: for all Israel were to come to Shechem to make him king.

And it came to pass, when Jeroboam the son of Nebat, who was yet in Egypt, heard *of it,* (for he was fled from the presence of king Solomon, and Jeroboam dwelt in Egypt;)

That they sent and called him. And Jeroboam and all the congregation of Israel came, and spake unto Rehoboam, saying,

Thy father made our yoke grievous: now therefore make thou the grievous service of thy father, and his heavy yoke which he put upon us, lighter, and we will serve thee.

And he said unto them, Depart yet *for* three days, then come again to me. And the people departed.

And king Rehoboam consulted with the old men, that stood before Solomon his father while he yet lived, and said, How do ye advise that I may answer this people?

And they spake unto him, saying, If thou will be a servant unto this people this day, and wilt serve them, and answer them, and speak good words to them, then they will be thy servants for ever.

But he forsook the counsel of the old men, which they had given him, and consulted with the young men that were grown up with him, *and* which stood before him.

And he said unto them, what counsel give ye that we may answer this people, who have spoken to me, saying, Make the yoke which thy father did put upon us lighter?

And the young men that were grown up with him spake unto him, saying, Thus shalt thou speak unto this people that spake unto thee, saying, Thy father made our yoke heavy, but make thou *it* lighter unto us; thus shalt thou say unto them, My little *finger* shall be thicker than my father's loins.

And now whereas my father did lade you with a heavy yoke, I will add to your yoke: my father hath chastised you with whips, but I will chastise you with scorpions.

So Jeroboam and all the people came to Rehoboam the third day, as the king had appointed, saying, Come to me again the third day.

And the king answered the people roughly, and forsook the old men's counsel that they gave him;

And spake to them after the counsel of the young men, saying, My father made your yoke heavy, and I will add to your yoke: my father *also* chastised you with whips, but I will chastise you with scorpions.

Wherefore the king hearkened not unto the people; for the cause was from the Lord, that he might perform his saying, which the Lord spake by Ahijah the Shilonite unto Jeroboam the son of Nebat.

So when all Israel saw that the king hearkened not unto them, the people answered the king, saying, What portion have we in David? neither *have we* inheritance in the son of Jesse: to your tents, O Israel: now see to thine own house, David. So Israel departed unto their tents.

I Kings 12:1-16

This is a beautiful story that shows us a man who would not embrace a new Time Zone of God. Rehoboam, the son of Solomon, went to Shechem to be made king. The congregation came to Rehoboam complaining about the oppression of the people and hoping for certain changes in the attitude of the kings of the house of David, since King Solomon was dead and there was a re-entry of a new Time Zone. Every time there is a new Time Zone, the old Zone and its activities must die for the new Zone to be embraced.

The congregation agreed to continue being ruled by the house of David, only if Rehoboam would lighten the burden placed upon the people by his father, Solomon. Rehoboam told them to depart and come again in three days for an answer. But within the process of time, he consulted two groups of people for advice. These were old men who were counselors to his famous father and the young men he grew up with. Listening carefully to the advice from the old men. *"If thou wilt be a servant unto this people this day, and wilt serve them, and answer them, and speak good words to them, then they will be thy servants for ever."* This was some of the wisest advice ever given to a king.

In other words, the old men advised Rehoboam to change the pattern of things and embrace the new Time Zone. But Rehoboam permitted the youth of the kingdom to cause him to make one of the greatest mistakes a ruler ever made. Through the *one choice* and wrong decision, many wars were fought, the kingdom was divided and, above all, his call to the kingship office was destroyed. Even though he continued to rule over Judah, a great chunk of the kingdom was rent away from him and given to Jeroboam. This is what happens when we refuse to embrace God's Time Zone. Rehoboam still preferred the old style under the reign of King Solomon, and this cost him his call and kingdom. We must be willing to embrace God's Time Zone and walk accordingly.

King Rehoboam's ministry was reduced. His members were divided. Some opted for the old move and its starchy ways, and many more opted for God's new Time Zone. It is dangerous not to move with God. It is dangerous not to embrace the new Zone of God. Ministries and churches that will not embrace God's new Zone will experience a great emigration of members to other churches and ministries.

Secondly, a refusal to embrace God's Time Zone will cause the favor of God to depart from your life, church and ministry, and create an opening for the enemy.

And it came to pass, after the year was expired, at the time when kings go forth *to battle*, that David sent Joab, and his servants with him, and all Israel; and they destroyed the children of Ammon, and besieged Rabbah. But David tarried still at Jerusalem.

And it came to pass in an eveningtide, that David arose from off his bed, and walked upon the roof of the king's house: and from the roof he saw a woman washing herself; and the woman *was* very beautiful to look upon.

And David sent and inquired after the woman. And *one* said, *Is* not this Bath-sheba, the daughter of Eliam, the wife of Uriah the Hittite?

And David sent messengers, and took her; and she came in unto him, and he lay with her; for she was purified from her uncleanness: and she returned unto her house.

II Samuel 11:1-4

Wherefore has thou despised the commandment of the Lord, to do evil in his sight? thou hast killed Uriah the Hittite with the sword, and hast taken his wife *to be* thy wife, and hast slain him with the sword of the children of Ammon.

Now therefore the sword shall never depart from thine house; because thou hast despised me, and hast taken the wife of Uriah the Hittite to be thy wife.

Thus saith the Lord, Behold, I will raise up evil against thee out of thine own house, and I will take thy wives before thine eyes, and give *them* unto thy neighbor, and he shall lie with thy wives in the sight of this sun.

For thou didst *it* **secretly: but I will do this thing before all Israel, and before the sun.**

And David said unto Nathan, I have sinned against the Lord. And Nathan said unto David, the Lord also hath put away thy sin; thou shalt not die.

II Samuel 12:9-13

David was in this predicament. His lack of embracing the Time Zone of God cost him the favor of God. At the time when he was supposed to embrace the "time of war," he was busy strolling upon his roof. This gave room for the spirit of lust to enter into his heart. Lust finally developed into the sin of adultery, lies and murder. David was supposed to be in the battlefield because it was "the time and season when kings go forth to battle." He was in the wrong place at the wrong time. His refusal to understand and flow with the time of war caused a curse to be released upon his household. "Now therefore the sword shall never depart from thine house; because thou hast despised me, and hast taken the wife of Uriah the Hittite to be thy wife."

The final danger is that you will become dry and starchy in your ways because you are operating in an old Time Zone with old weapons.

Chapter X

The Rewards for Embracing
God's Time Zone

Just as there are dangers of not embracing God's Zone, there are rewards for embracing God's Time Zone.

And I will restore to you the years that the locust hath eaten, the cankerworm, and the caterpillar, and the palmerworm, my great army which I sent among you.

Joel 2:25

The first reward is the reward of restoration and revival. As we move into God's new Time Zone, we will begin to experience restoration in our lives and ministry. Restoration is the causing to return to a former position or condition by renewing or returning that which has been taken away. The biblical concept of restoration comprises the work of God, and to restore the individual believer to the image of God.

And he shall send Jesus Christ, which before was preached unto you:

Whom the heaven must receive until the times of restitution of all things, which God hath spoken by the mouth of all his holy prophets since the world began.

Acts 3:20-21

Here we see the importance of restoration to the Church. Jesus is literally held in the heavens "... until the times of restitution (restoration) of all things, which God hath spoken by the mouth of all His holy prophets since the world began." Christ is kept by the Father from returning again, until those things lost by the early Church and spoken by the prophets are restored to Her. The time of restoration thus precedes the second coming of Christ. Notice, also, that the passage speaks about "times" of restoration. There are different times and seasons of divine restoration.

Secondly, embracing God's new Time Zone will produce fresh new directions for God's people.

> **And it came to pass, when David and his men were come to Ziklag on the third day; that the Amalekites had invaded the south, and Ziglag, and smitten Ziklag, and burned it with fire;**
>
> **And had taken the women captives, that *were* therein: they slew not any; either great or small, but carried *them* away, and went on their way.**
>
> **So David and his men came to the city, and, behold, *it was* burned with fire; and their wives, and their sons, and their daughters, were taken captives.**
>
> **Then David and the people that *were* with him lifted up their voices and wept, until they had no more power to weep.**
>
> **And David said to Abiathar the priest, Ahimelech's son, I pray thee; bring me hither the ephod. And Abiathar brought thither the ephod to David.**
>
> **And David inquired at the Lord, saying, Shall I pursue after this troop? shall I overtake them? And he answered him, Pursue: for thou shalt surely overtake *them*, and without fail recover *all*.**
>
> **And David recovered all that the Amalekites had carried away: and David rescued his two wives.**
>
> **I Samuel 30:1-4,7-8,18**

David, after his return to Ziklag and discovery that the women were taken captive, wept with his men until they had no more power. But in order to receive a fresh new direction concerning what to do, David had to discern and embrace God's new Time Zone. He inquired from God on the proper timing to pursue the enemy. He wanted to understand God's launching time. He was flexible and ready to move with God's direction. And when he received the answer, "Pursue: for thou shalt surely overtake them, and without fail recover all." David quickly embraced God's timing by pursuing the enemy, and the Bible says that, "David recovered all that the Amalekites had carried away: and David rescued his two wives."

Finally, it will cause the Body of Christ to enter into divine prosperity. They are not experiencing divine prosperity. Many believers are not experiencing divine prosperity because they are operating the financial strategies of old Zones. God, in this hour, is causing financial revelation to come upon the Church in order for the Body of Christ to experience a breakthrough — a sudden burst of knowledge that will take you past the place and point of resistance.

Chapter XI

How to Move into God's Time Zones

I believe it is the desire of many Christians today to move and flow into God's new Time Zone. But having just a desire is not enough. We must move in there. Where? God's Time Zone! But in order to do this, there are certain things that we must do and consider.

Winds of Change

The first, most important, way of moving into God's Time Zone is *"moving with the winds of change."* Change is inevitable in this hour. In order for us to embrace God's new Zone, we must respond properly to the winds of change.

The glory of this latter house shall be greater than of the former, saith the Lord of hosts: and in this place will I give peace, saith the Lord of hosts.

Haggai 2:9

God has promised us what this new Time Zone will look like. He said it would be greater than the latter house. Which house? All of God's prior Zones. But in order to experience this greater move of the Spirit of God, the Body of Christ must be willing to change. We must change our ways, our styles of operation, our attitudes and our styles of life. We must repent from our wicked ways and turn ourselves over to God to make us, all over again. Many Christians desire the glory, but yet refuse to change with the movement of God.

151

And the Lord said to Samuel, Behold, I will do a thing in Israel, at which both the ears of every one that heareth it shall tingle.

I Samuel 3:11

The same thing happened to the house of Eli. They would not change from their evil ways. Every time God desires to do a new thing, the first thing He does is to demand a change. The Body of Christ will not receive the NEW until the OLD is let go of, and this is what God is calling for in this hour. Because of the new things that are about to happen, God is calling for an immediate change within the Body of Christ. Since Eli and his household refused to change, they were not candidates for the new *thing*. Change brings the new. That is why the Lord spoke to Samuel and said, "Behold, I will do a *new thing* in Israel, at which both the ears of every one that heareth it shall tingle." God is saying these same words today to the Church. He wants to do a new thing and the ears of everyone that heareth of this new movement of God will know that it is the doing of the Lord.

For before these days there was no hire for man, nor any hire for beast; neither *was there any* peace to him that went out or came in because of the affliction: for I set all men everyone against his neighbour.

But now I *will* not *be* unto the residue of this people as in the former days, saith the Lord of hosts.

For the seed *shall be* prosperous; the vine shall give her fruit, and the ground shall give her increase, and the heavens shall give their dew; and I will cause the remnant of this people to possess all these *things*.

Zechariah 8:10-12

Zechariah prophetically began to talk about the new move of God in His Time Zone. He talked of the previous days (the old Zones), of how there were no hire for men and beast, and how men were set against their

152

neighbor. He was talking about God's previous Zones, and the sins and atrocities practiced. But then, prophetically, he began to talk about God's new Time Zone. He said, "but *now* I will not be unto the residue (remnant) of His people as in the former days ...." This is the prophet Zechariah prophesying about God's new Time Zone. He said for the seed of this new Zone shall be prosperous, their vine shall give her fruit, the ground shall give increase and I will cause the remnant of this people to possess all things. Hallelujah! This is the promise for God's people in this hour. But for this to happen, we must move with the winds of change.

Past Accomplishments versus New Accomplishments

The second vital way to move into God's new Time Zone is by learning to put past accomplishments behind and striving for new accomplishments in God's Time Zone. It is a common occurrence within the Body of Christ to hear Christians glory about past accomplishments and past defeats. Many believers remember when God use to do "so and so" in their lives. But now the "so and so" is over. Dwelling on past accomplishments will put you in a complacent state and stupor. God is calling for believers who will dare to launch into the new.

But what things were gain to me, those I counted loss for Christ.

Yea doubtless, and I count all things *but* loss for the excellency of the knowledge of Christ Jesus my Lord: for whom I have suffered the loss of all things, and do count them *but* dung, that I may win Christ.

Brethren, I count not myself to have apprehended: but *this* one thing *I do* forgetting those things which are behind, and reaching forth unto those things which are before.

I press toward the mark of the prize of the high calling of God in Christ Jesus.

Let therefore, as many as be perfect, be thus minded: and if in any thing ye be otherwise minded, God shall reveal even this unto you.

Philippians 3:7-8,13-15

Paul understood this very key ingredient. He knew that glorying in the past accomplishment would put him in a comfort Zone and kill his zeal of striving. Many Christians' zeal of striving has been killed because of remaining in the comfort Zones of their accomplishments. But Paul made it clear, the things that I have accomplished, "I counted loss for Christ." But Paul knew that glorying in his accomplishment would prevent him from embracing God's Zones and refreshings. He counted everything loss for Christ. That is what we must do to fully embrace God's Time Zone. We count every great and small accomplishment as loss. We must not create an idol out of them. Instead, we must strive earnestly for something new from the presence of God, never satisfied until there is a new refreshing.

I love what Paul said in verse 13. He said, "brethren." We are "brethren" and he is talking to us. Paul said, *"I count not myself to have apprehended: but this one thing I do, forgetting those things which are behind, and reaching forth unto those things which are before."* Isn't this powerful? Paul, with his great resume, talked about forgetting the past and to reach forth and embrace those things in God's new Time Zone. He desired to press for the prize and not just for the mark. There is a prize! All of God's people must desire and press for this prize. Not just to get to the mark, but striving to win a prize. But for this to happen, the Body of Christ must be willing to embrace the various Time Zones of God that come before our departure to heaven. Paul's last counseling on this is very interesting. He said, *"therefore as many as be matured, be thus minded."* In other words, if you are a matured believer, you have a responsibility *to forget* the past accomplishments and to press for the prize. The words "to forget" here, from its original meaning literally means "to have no remembrance and recollections of past events, experiences and achievements." In other words, it means to develop amnesia for the past.

Associations

Be ye not unequally yoked together with unbelievers: for what fellowship hath righteousness with unrighteousness? and what communion hath light with darkness?

And what concord hath Christ with Belial? or what part hath he that believeth with an infidel?

And what agreement hath the temple of God with idols? for ye are the temple of the living God; as God hath said, I will dwell in them, and walk in *them*; and I will be their God, and they shall be my people.

II Corinthians 6:14-16

The third way is through association. The right association will influence and assist you in embracing God's new Time Zone. This is an area that most Christians take for granted. We must be careful who our associates are. Your associate, whether good or bad, has a fifty-percent chance of influencing you towards something. Paul knew this. That was why he said to the Corinthian Church, *"be not unequally yoked."* Many believers think that being unequally yoked is just related to the unbelievers. You can be unequally yoked in doctrines and beliefs. You can be unequally yoked by associating with Christians that are not walking in line with the precepts and commandments of God. It is very easy for a believer, who understands the timing of God, to influence another believer concerning God's divine schedules. But it would be difficult for that same individual to influence another believer who does not believe in God's timetable. So, you see why it is very important to associate yourself with the right people. Before associating, prayerfully find out if God wants you to connect yourself with that individual or not.

155

Wrong Association

And, behold, there came a man of God out of Judah by the word of the Lord unto Bethel: and Jeroboam stood by the alter to burn incense.

And it came to pass, when king Jeroboam heard the saying of the man of God, which had cried against the altar in Bethel, that he put forth his hand from the altar, saying, Lay hold on him. And his hand, which he put forth against him, dried up, so that he could not pull it in again to him.

And the king said unto the man of God, Come home with me, and refresh thyself, and I will give thee a reward.

And the man of God said unto the king, if thou wilt give me half thine house, I will not go in with thee, neither will I eat bread nor drink water in this place:

For so was it charged me by the word of the Lord, saying, Eat no bread, nor drink water, nor turn again by the same way that thou camest.

Now there dwelt an old prophet in Bethel; and his sons came and told him all the works that the man of God had done that day in Bethel: the words which he had spoken unto the king, them they told also to their father.

And their father said unto them, What way went he? For his sons had seen what way the man of God went, which came from Judah.

Then he said unto him, Come home with me, and eat bread.

And he said, I may not return with thee, nor go in with thee: neither will I eat bread nor drink water with thee in this place:

For it was said to me by the word of the Lord, Thou shalt eat no bread nor drink water there, nor turn again to go by the way that thou camest.

He said unto him, I *am* a prophet also as thou *art*; and an angel spake unto me by the word of the Lord, saying, Bring him back with thee into thine house, that he may eat bread and drink water. *But* he lied unto him.

So he went back with him, and did eat bread in his house, and drank water.

And it came to pass, as they sat at the table, that the word of the Lord came unto the prophet that brought him back:

And he cried unto the man of God that came from Judah, saying, Thus saith the Lord, Forasmuch as thou hast disobeyed the mouth of the Lord, and hast not kept the commandment which the Lord thy God commanded thee,

But camest back, and hast eaten bread and drunk water in the place, of the which *the* Lord did say to thee, Eat no bread, and drink no water; thy carcass shall not come unto the sepulchre of thy fathers.

I Kings 13:1,4,7-9,11-12,15-22

This is a good example of the penalty paid when you associate with the wrong people. The prophet from Judah was specifically instructed by God not to associate with anybody, eat nor drink during his mission. He knew this. And even after the demonstration of the power of God through him in restoring the withered hand of Jeroboam and Jeroboam's persuasion for the prophet to come home with him to eat and receive a reward, he flatly refused, because he realized the commandment of God.

But it was a different issue, when the old prophet from Bethel appeared on the scene. We need to be very careful of those believers in the Body of Christ who claim to know, when actually they don't know anything. Many have wrongly associated themselves with people who parade themselves as spiritual or gifted, and yet act like "Spanky and the Little Rascals." Looks and words will deceive you. You need some fruits and a divine direction.

157

The prophet from Judah fell into this predicament. He was persuaded to associate himself with the old prophet, simply because the old prophet said he was a prophet. The young prophet from Judah paid dearly for this with his life. This is not play stuff. It is real. Your associates will either increase you or decrease you. The old prophet lied, so that the young prophet would associate with him. "Church, watch out!" In order to embrace this movement of God, we will have to sever some of our associations that will do everything possible to prevent us from serving the purpose of God for our lives.

Seeking the Lord

The fourth way is by seeking the Lord. God's own divine schedule of shakening is moving to seeking Him. As never before, the Church must be in the place called "there" to seek the Lord. David was a leader who knew, understood and sought the Lord for everything he did. He was a man who knew how to inquire of the Lord. He inquired of the Lord concerning everything.

Then they told David, saying, Behold, the Philistines fight against Keilah, and they rob the threshingfloors.

Therefore David inquired of the Lord, saying, Shall I go and smite these Philistines? And the Lord said unto David, Go, and smite the Philistines, and save Keilah.

And David's men said unto him, Behold, we be afraid here in Judah: how much more then if we come to Keilah; against the armies of the Philistines?

Then David inquired of the Lord yet again. And the Lord answered him and said, Arise, go down to Keilah: for I will deliver the Philistines into thine hand.

So David and his men went to Keilah, and fought with the Philistines, and brought away their cattle, and smote them with a great slaughter. So David save the inhabitants of Keilah.

And it was told Saul, that David was come to Keilah. And Saul said, God hath delivered him into mine hand; for he is shut in, by entering into a town that hath gates and bars.

And Saul called all the people together to war, to go down to Keilah, to besiege David and his men.

And David knew that Saul secretly practiced mischief against him; and he said to Abiathar the priest, Bring hither the ephod.

Then said David, O Lord God of Israel, thy servant hath certainly heard that Saul seeketh to come to Keilah, to destroy the city for my sake.

Will the men of Keilah deliver me up into his hand? will Saul come down, as thy servant hath heard? O Lord God of Israel, I beseech thee, tell thy servant. And the Lord said, He will come down.

Then said David, Will the men of Keilah deliver me and my men into the hand of Saul? And the Lord said, They will deliver *thee* up.

The David and his men, *which were* about six hundred, arose and departed out of Keilah, and went whithersoever they could go. And it was told Saul that David was escaped from Keilah; and he forebare to go forth.

I Samuel 23:1-5,7-13

And it came to pass after this, that David inquired of the Lord, saying, Shall I go up into any of the cities of Judah? And the Lord said unto him, Go up. And David said, Whither shall I go up? And he said, Unto Hebron.

II Samuel 2:1

When they told David that the Philistines were attacking Keilah, he did not just rush into battle against the Philistines. The first thing he did was to inquire of the Lord. He wanted God's strategy. God's opinion meant much more to him than any man's opinion. Every time he inquired of the Lord, God always answered him. It is not surprising that he was called a man after God's heart. He knew how and when to invoke the presence of the Lord. Notice carefully, before he embraced the "time of war" with the Philistines, he first of all made sure that he sought the Lord. Seeking brings direction, strategy and victory.

The same happened after the death of Saul and Jonathan. David inquired of the Lord what to do. He did not just move with his families to Judah. He first of all sought the Lord. He was concerned about what God had to say. This must also be of great concern to us. In order to fully embrace God's new Time Zone in this hour, we must be a people that inquire of God and seek him in everything we do.

*M*y dear friend, before you lay this book aside, make sure God is first in your life and you are in the right position with Him. In order to guarantee this, let's confess the following together.

1. **Before God, I Confess That I Am a Sinner** For all have sinned and fall short of the glory of God.

Romans 3:23

2. **I Now Repent (Turn Around) Of My Sin And Come To The Lord Jesus Christ** Repent, then, and turn to God, so that your sins may be wiped out.

Acts 3:19

3. **I Accept Jesus As My Personal Savior And Lord** Yet to all who received him, to those who believed in his name, he gave the right to become children of God.

John 1:12

4. **I Thank The Lord, Jesus, For Dying For Me And Bearing Away My Sin** But God demonstrates his own love for us in this: While we were still sinners, Christ died for us.

Romans 5:8

5. **I Believe That Jesus Rose Again From The Dead: I Will Confess Him Before Men As My Lord** That if you confess with your mouth, "Jesus is Lord," and believe in your heart that God raised him from the dead, you will be saved.

Romans 10:9

"I believe I'm now born again, because the Word of God says I am! Jesus is now my Lord. Thank you, Jesus, for a new life and for saving me. I'm now a new person and a child of God. In Jesus' name, Amen!"

Have You Read
John Tetsola's Previous Book?
"DEVELOPING SPIRITUAL ACCURACY & PINPOINTING"

This book is a provoking tool for individuals who are
seeking to become Precise and Free from Spiritual Error.

This book, also brings clarity to understanding the various
changes we will encounter, by flowing with God's Spirit.

To order your copy of this inspirational book today (for just $9.⁹⁵),
use the order form enclosed in this book for your convenience.

Ecclesia Word Ministries, Inc.
P.O. Box 743
Bronx, New York 10462

To Order By Mail:

Name _____

Address _____

City _____ State _____

Zip _____ Phone (_____) _____

Qty.	Title Of Book	Donation	Total
	Developing Spiritual Accuracy & Pinpointing	$10.00	
	Understanding the Time Zones of God	$10.00	
	The Cave of Adullam: *A Type and Shadow of God's Prophetic Church Today*	$9.00	
	The Making Process of God's Prophetic Leaders	$9.00	

To Order By Phone Call: (718) 863-1834	Subtotal		
	Shipping		
	Total		

Shipping		
Order	**U.S.**	**Foreign**
$0 - $10	$2.00	12%
11 - 50	$3.00	of
51 - 100	$4.00	Gross
101 - up	5%	

Bookstores:

Call For Volume Discounts

— *Allow 3 to 4 Weeks For Delivery* —